SWEET
SENSATIONS

Virginia Hill & Lorna Garden

SWEET SENSATIONS

Delicious and healthy desserts
- for people with diabetes
- for weight control, and good health

Thanks to Eron Weir for recipe development assistance.

Thomas C. Lothian Pty Ltd
11 Munro Street, Port Melbourne, Victoria 3207

National Library of Australia
Cataloguing-in-Publication data:

Hill, Virginia.
 Sweet sensations : delicious desserts for people with
 diabetes for weight control and good health.
 Includes index
 ISBN 0 85091 992 4.
 1. Low-fat diet – Recipes. 2. Diabetes – Diet therapy –
 Recipes. 3. Desserts. I. Garden, Lorna. II. Title.
641.56314

Cover and text design by Jo Waite Design
Cover photographs by Sonya Pletes
Food styling designed by Janet Lillie
Printed in Australia by Southwood Press Pty Limited

Front cover: Summer Berry Risotto
Back cover: Hazelnut Chocolate Cheesecake

CONTENTS

Cheating with Chocolate

Fruits

Breakfasts & Brunches

INTRODUCTION

Over the years, while conducting cooking classes and talking with people, we have observed many of them cutting down on their intake of entrées and main dishes in order to indulge in the full complement of desserts and cakes.

Desserts and sweets are still considered indulgences by most people and are often associated with guilt and 'breaking the diet'. Given that the emphasis at the end of the twentieth century centres on a balanced diet, is our attitude toward these goodies a little harsh?

A balanced diet incorporates the philosophy of including a wide variety of foods for good health, with more of the nutritious foods and fewer of the less nutrient dense choices. This doesn't necessarily mean having less dessert, but instead choosing healthier options or modifying old favourites. With the many delicious low-fat dairy foods available today, this is not as difficult as you may think.

Reducing saturated fats is one of our strongest nutrition messages for minimising the risk of heart disease, cancer, diabetes and obesity. Unfortunately foods high in saturated fats such as butter, cream, soft cheeses and chocolate feature strongly in traditional desserts. Combined with sugar, fats carry and bring out unique flavours in food, so eliminating fats totally makes for bland, unappetising food. Fat is also essential for many functions in the body, and evidence is mounting that particular fats (such as omega-3 polyunsaturated fats) may have a number of real health benefits.

In *Sweet Sensations* we have aimed to produce delicious desserts that are low in saturated fats and have used poly- and monounsaturated fats where necessary. We have avoided the use of large amounts of added sugar in most recipes by using fresh fruits and other naturally sweet foods.

If you are one of the many Australians aiming to control body weight, reduce the risk of heart disease and cancer, stay healthy with diabetes, or you simply want to keep fit and healthy and perform at your peak, this is the book for you.

Virginia Hill

SWEET
and NUTRITIOUS

Sweet Sensations is written for people with diabetes who
aim to eat like healthy people without diabetes. It is
written for the many people (with and without diabetes)
who want to keep weight and blood cholesterol levels
down, and maintain a fit and healthy lifestyle, but still
enjoy their food.

With current research breaking new ground in the
area of diet and diabetes, the dietary restrictions of old
are being replaced rapidly with a more liberal and
individual approach. Researchers are gathering more
information each day on the glycaemic index (G.I.) of
foods, that is, the effect of a carbohydrate food on blood
glucose levels compared to an equal amount of glucose.
The glycaemic index highlights the importance of the
type of carbohydrate food rather than simply the
quantity of carbohydrate consumed each day. Low G.I.
foods have been demonstrated to help control blood
sugar (glucose) levels in people with diabetes. The G.I.
opens the door for the inclusion of many foods that
were previously considered 'forbidden' by people with
diabetes. For example, we now know that most people
with diabetes can include small amounts of sugar in
their diet, and that some foods containing sugar actually

give a lower blood glucose response than some starchy foods.

People who have had diabetes for many years may find it astonishing that *Sweet Sensations* is a cookbook for people with diabetes. Indeed it can just as well be a book for weight control, a healthy heart or many other health reasons. There are no portions or exchanges, very few artificial sweeteners, and you will even find the occasional chocolate and other indulgence foods.

Let me highlight some nutrition facts that were important to us in the development of *Sweet Sensations* recipes.

- Diet for people with diabetes should be based on low-fat and low glycaemic index, carbohydrate-containing foods.*
- The amount of carbohydrate you require each day varies considerably between individuals, depending on activity level, age, blood sugar control, and blood lipid levels.
- Including some sugar in your diet will generally not upset overall diabetic control and may make it easier to adhere to a low-fat diet.*
- Saturated fat intake should be kept low; however, the inclusion of monounsaturated fats may help with blood glucose and blood cholesterol control.
- Regularly monitoring your blood glucose levels is the best way to determine which foods and recipes allow best blood glucose control.
- Regular exercise is a great way to improve diabetic control, and improve health and fitness, and to justify more healthy desserts and snacks!

Based on this knowledge, we have formulated delicious sweet dishes that include in their ingredients low glycaemic index choices such as low-fat dairy foods, basmati rice, pasta, sweet potato, and fruit. We have aimed to include a large variety of fruits throughout *Sweet Sensations* for a number of reasons. Fruit provides

---

* *Diabetes Today*, Autumn 98, p. 11.

sugar in the form of fructose, which is a particularly sweet sugar. In fruit the sugar is found in combination with dietary fibre and other components that can help slow down the rate at which sugar is absorbed into the bloodstream. Fruits with a low glycaemic index, such as apples, apricots, bananas, cherries, oranges, peaches, pears, plums and dried fruits, are particularly useful foods to include for people with diabetes or poor blood sugar control.

Fruit provides the soluble fibre pectin that may help reduce blood cholesterol levels and the risk of heart disease. Fruit also contains valuable antioxidants, such as vitamin C and flavonoids, which are believed to be protective against heart disease and certain cancers. The other great beauty of fruit is that most varieties are fat free, and, like all plant foods, they contain no cholesterol.

We have used small amounts of sugar and honey to add sweetness, rather than artificial sweeteners, which invariably leave a bitter aftertaste when cooked. It is also our aim to provide higher-fibre options through the use of fruit, wholemeal products, nuts and seeds.

Our recipes use only small amounts of margarine and oils, and we encourage you to choose mono-unsaturated varieties of these. Look for canola margarine and canola and olive oils for cooking.

> **Note:** Nutritional analyses are approximate only, and were calculated using the Australian Commonwealth Government Nutab 95 figures.

When using the nutritional data for each recipe, it is important that you recognise the serve size of the dish. The portions suggested will provide only small amounts of added sugar, and most people with diabetes will find they can enjoy them, and keep good blood glucose control.

So sweet is no longer a dirty word. It's time to add a touch of taste to your desserts, snacks and condiments. Remember to discuss your individual dietary require-ments with your dietitian and doctor, and monitor your blood glucose levels regularly.

Lorna Garden, BSc Dip.Diet.APD
Consultant Dietitian

CAKES & PASTRY

CAKES & PASTRY

Fresh from the oven cakes are hard to resist.

Here are a few tips for successful baking.

Conventionally baked cakes need to be fully cooked before removing from the oven to avoid sinking. There are several ways to gauge if a cake is cooked. A cooked cake will bounce back when touched lightly in the centre with the fingertip, and will come away from the sides of the tin. A skewer inserted in the centre of the cake will come out clean and dry.

If a cake cracks and rises to a peak in the centre, the tin may be too small for the quantity of mixture; the cake was cooked in an oven that was too hot; or, for ovens that are not fan-forced, the cake may have been placed too high in the oven.

Microwave cakes are easy and quick to make, taking just a few minutes. They are moist and tender if not overcooked. Here are a few tips to help you achieve the best results if you have never baked cakes before in your microwave oven.

Cakes do not brown or develop a crust during microwave cooking, so top with a sauce, fruit, toasted coconut or finely ground nuts for an attractive finish.

Line microwave-safe cake dishes with paper towels rather than greasing and sugaring. Fat and sugar heat quickly and divert microwaves away from the cake batter.

Fill cake containers no more than half full, as microwave cakes expand more than conventionally cooked ones.

Cakes cook better in round dishes than in square ones. A special microwave cake-ring ensures cakes cook in the time given in recipes.

Allow the batter to rest for 5–10 minutes after preparation. This helps the top of the cake cook more evenly.

Cakes cook best if elevated so that microwaves can penetrate from underneath the container. They also need moving several times during cooking to ensure an even result. If you open the oven door during cooking the cake will not fall as microwave ovens cook by power and not heat.

Refrigerate baked cakes to keep them fresh. Most cakes can be frozen whole in microwave-safe bags, or as individual slices in plastic wrap.

Apricot & Hazelnut Bran Cake

*If fibre is what you need in your diet, this is the ideal cake. Serve it with **Apricot Sauce** (page 186).*

Energy: 820 kJ/195 kCal
Fat: 6 g
Carbohydrate: 28 g
Fibre: 8 g

Consume plenty of fluids each day with a high-fibre diet to ensure a healthy bowel.

Variation

Try dried figs in place of peaches.

Makes 8–10 slices

spray oil

1 cup low-fat milk

1 cup All Bran cereal

$3/4$ cup self-raising wholemeal flour

2 tbsp brown sugar

1 cup each chopped dried peaches and apricots

2 tbsp crushed hazelnuts

1 tsp bicarbonate of soda

CONVENTIONAL

1 Preheat the oven to 180°C. Spray a loaf tin or square cake tin with oil and line with baking paper.
2 Combine the milk and All Bran in a mixing bowl. Soak for 5–10 minutes.
3 Add the flour, brown sugar, dried fruit, hazelnuts and bicarbonate of soda. Mix well.
4 Pour into the pan and bake for 40–45 minutes.

Apple & Pecan Cake

Served warm from the oven, this classic cake becomes a heaven-sent dessert.

Serves 6–8

1 cup wholemeal self-raising flour

$^1/_2$ cup oats

1 tsp bicarbonate of soda

1 tsp allspice

2 tbsp brown sugar

$^1/_2$ cup pecans

$^1/_3$ cup oil

1 (55 g) egg, lightly beaten

2 apples, peeled, cored and chopped

Energy:	740 kJ/175 kCal
Fat:	10 g
Carbohydrate:	18 g
Fibre:	3 g

CONVENTIONAL

1 Preheat the oven to 180°C. Lightly grease and line a 20 cm cake tin with baking paper.
2 In a bowl combine the flour, oats, bicarbonate of soda, allspice, sugar and pecans.
3 Make a well in the centre, then add the oil and egg. Add the apples and combine well.
4 Pour into the prepared tin and cook for 35 minutes until golden brown.

Yoghurt & Banana Cake

Banana cake is an old favourite, popular with everyone from 1 to 100. It's easy to make and eat.

Serves 10–12

200 ml vanilla low-fat yoghurt

2 very ripe bananas, mashed

1 cup self-raising flour, sifted

$^1/_3$ cup wholemeal self-raising flour, sifted

2 (55 g) eggs, separated

1$^1/_2$ tsp baking powder

1 tbsp castor sugar

1 tbsp desiccated coconut, toasted

Energy:	630 kJ/150 kCal
Fat:	2 g
Carbohydrate:	28 g
Fibre:	2 g

Rich in fibre and protein, this moist cake is also very low in fat.

CONVENTIONAL

1 Preheat the oven to 180°C. Lightly grease a 20 cm pan.
2 In a mixing bowl combine the yoghurt, bananas, flours, egg yolks and baking powder.
3 In a separate bowl beat the egg whites until soft peaks form. Add the sugar and beat until combined. Fold the egg whites into the banana mixture in two batches.
4 Pour into the prepared pan, and bake for 30 minutes. Sprinkle with coconut, slice and serve with yoghurt.

MICROWAVE

1 Spray a 23 cm microwave-safe ring mould with cooking oil.
2 In a mixing bowl combine the yoghurt, bananas, flours, egg yolks and baking powder.
3 In a separate bowl beat the egg whites until soft peaks form. Add the sugar and beat until combined. Fold the egg whites into the banana mixture in two batches.
4 Pour into the prepared mould, and cook on MEDIUM HIGH (70–80%) for 8 minutes, elevated, turning halfway during the cooking time. Allow to stand for 4 minutes before turning out onto a wire rack to cool. Sprinkle with coconut, slice and serve with yoghurt.

Variation

Add 2 tbsp of finely chopped pecans or macadamias.

Hint

If you have any overripe bananas, avoid waste by placing them in the freezer to store for whenever mashed bananas are required. After thawing no mashing is required as they are already mushy.

Moist Mango Cake

A refreshing sweet surprise that is delightful served with yoghurt.
It's handy to have on hand if you have a group of people to feed.

Makes 12 slices

2 mangoes or 800 g canned mango, drained

$1/2$ cup almond meal

$1/4$ cup rice flour

$1/2$ cup self-raising flour

$1/4$ cup castor sugar

1 tsp baking powder

2 (55 g) eggs

3 egg whites

1 tbsp shredded coconut (optional)

Energy:	325 kJ/75 kCal
Fat:	3 g
Carbohydrate:	9 g
Fibre:	1 g

Mangoes are rich in vitamins C and A, important antioxidants and provide natural sweetness and moisture in cakes and muffins.

CONVENTIONAL

1 Preheat the oven to 180°C. Lightly grease and line a 20 cm cake pan.

2 Puree the mango flesh and measure out 2 cups. Set aside.

3 Place the almond meal, rice flour, self-raising flour, sugar and baking powder in a food processor and process for 30 seconds. Pour in the mango puree and process until well combined. Add the eggs, one at a time, and process until combined.

4 In a clean bowl whisk the egg whites until stiff peaks form and fold into the mango mixture.

5 Pour the batter into the pan and bake for 1 hour. You may need to cover the cake with foil halfway through cooking to prevent the cake from browning too much.

6 Cool, sprinkle with coconut, and serve with vanilla-flavoured yoghurt.

Variation

Canned peaches may be used in place of the mango.

Hint

Peeled and cubed fresh mango freezes well.

Carrot Cake with Cream Cheese Topping

A moist cake that makes an excellent snack for hungry school kids or active people. It keeps in the refrigerator for a few days and freezes well.

Serves 12

spray oil

3 cups grated carrot, approximately
    3 medium-sized carrots or
    5 small carrots

1/2 cup grated apple

1/2 cup canola oil

2/3 cup raisins

2 tbsp dark brown sugar

1 cup wholemeal flour, sifted

1 cup plain flour, sifted

1 tsp baking powder

3 egg whites

Topping

125 g light cream cheese

1/2 tbsp honey

1/2 tsp cinnamon

1/2 tsp ground ginger

Energy: 930 kJ/222 kCal
Fat: 10 g
Carbohydrate: 27 g
Fibre: 3 g

The old wives' tale that carrots are good for your eyes is true. Carrots contain the pigment betacarotene, which converts into vitamin A in the body and is needed for maintaining eyesight.

CONVENTIONAL

1 Preheat the oven to 160°C. Spray a 20 cm cake tin with oil and line with baking paper.
2 Place the carrots, apple, oil, raisins and sugar in a mixing bowl.
3 Add the flours and baking powder and mix well.
4 Whisk the egg whites to firm peaks and fold into the mixture in two batches until combined.
5 Spoon into the tin and bake for 1 hour.
6 To make the topping, beat the cream cheese with an electric beater. Add the honey and beat until light and creamy. Add the cinnamon and ginger, and mix until combined. Spread over the cooled cake.

MICROWAVE

1 Spray a 23 cm microwave-safe ring mould lightly with cooking oil.
2 Place the carrots, apple, oil, raisins and sugar in a mixing bowl.
3 Add the flours and baking powder and mix well.
4 Whisk the egg whites to firm peaks and fold into the mixture in two batches until combined.
5 Spoon into the mould and cook on MEDIUM HIGH (70–80%) for 13 minutes, elevated, rotating every 4 minutes during the cooking time. Allow to stand for 4 minutes before turning out onto a wire rack to cool.

Poppyseed Cupcakes

Poppyseeds have a nutty taste, and are popular in Europe and the Middle East for flavouring patisserie. While we use them to sprinkle over bread rolls, they are also a good complement to orange cakes and muffins.

Makes 12 cupcakes or 18 small cupcakes

1 cup self-raising flour

$^1/_2$ cup almond meal

1 tbsp custard powder

2 tbsp poppyseeds

zest of 1 large orange or tangelo

3 egg whites

$^3/_4$ cup skim milk

$1^1/_2$ tbsp **Three-fruit Marmalade** (page 171)

Energy:	300 kJ/70 kCal
Fat:	2 g
Carbohydrate:	11 g
Fibre:	1 g

CONVENTIONAL

1 Preheat the oven to 200°C. Lightly grease a muffin pan.
2 In a bowl mix together the flour, almond meal, custard powder, poppyseeds and zest.
3 In a clean bowl beat the egg whites until stiff, and fold into the dry mixture.
4 Add the milk and stir until combined.
5 Spoon the mixture into the muffin pan. Bake for 15 minutes, or until golden brown.
6 Glaze with marmalade while still warm.

Variation

Toasted sesame seeds can be used in place of poppyseeds.

Pumpkin & Coconut Flan

Pumpkin is a versatile member of the squash family. It can be added to bread scones, puddings, pies or cakes.

Makes 16 thin wedges

400 g pumpkin, peeled and seeds removed

$^1/_4$ cup water

$^3/_4$ cup self-raising flour

2 tbsp rice flour

3 tbsp desiccated coconut

2 tbsp coconut milk powder

1 (60 g) egg

3 tbsp oil

$^1/_4$ cup castor sugar

Energy:	430 kJ/105 kCal
Fat:	4 g
Carbohydrate:	14 g
Fibre:	1 g

Just the right amount of carbohydrate for a snack to keep the energy levels up.

MICROWAVE

1 Lightly grease and line a 23 cm microwave-safe flan dish with paper towels.

2 Place the pumpkin and water in a microwave-safe bowl and cook on HIGH (100%) for 7–8 minutes. Do not strain off the water. Mash and allow to cool. (The pumpkin must be quite a runny mash.)

3 In a mixing bowl combine the flour, rice flour, coconut and coconut milk powder.

4 In a separate bowl mix together the egg, oil, sugar and cooled mashed pumpkin.

5 Gradually add the flour mixture to the pumpkin and stir until combined.

6 Pour into the prepared dish and spread out evenly. Cover and cook on MEDIUM HIGH (70–80%) for 5–6 minutes. Allow to stand for 10–15 minutes to cool, then remove from the dish.

7 Serve the cake warm with **Custard** (page 182) as a dessert or dusted with coconut for afternoon tea. Be sure to cut the pieces smaller when serving for afternoon tea, as the cake is quite sticky.

Hint

Pumpkin seeds make an interesting garnish as well as being a nutritious snack.

Berry Tofu Torte

Tofu has been in existence for 2500 years. It is made from soybeans, one of the oldest plants used by humans. Tofu is highly nutritious, is an excellent source of protein, and provides calcium, iron and unsaturated fats.

Serves 12

Base

12 wheat-style biscuits

$^1/_3$ cup water

Energy: 560 kJ/135 kCal
Fat: 8 g
Carbohydrate: 15 g
Fibre: 0.5 g

Tofu and other soybean products contain phytoestrogens, which may help reduce menopausal symptoms in some women and are believed to have a number of other health benefits.

Topping

1 (375 g) packet tofu, drained

1 (425 g) can raspberries, drained and juices reserved

$^1/_4$ cup castor sugar

2 tbsp lemon juice

$^1/_3$ cup self-raising flour

CONVENTIONAL

1 Preheat the oven to 180°C. Lightly oil a 20 cm springform pan.
2 For the base, crush the biscuits in a food processor until a fine crumb forms. Add the water, combine, and press into the tin. Refrigerate until the topping is ready.
3 For the topping, in a food processor beat the tofu until smooth. Add the sugar, lemon juice and flour. Combine until smooth, then fold in the strained raspberries.
4 Pour the topping over the biscuit base. Spread smoothly.
5 Bake for 40 minutes until the mixture is set and a skewer inserted in the centre comes out clean.
6 When cool, serve with the raspberry juices drizzled over the top.

Beetroot Cake

This cake is moist and easy to make, with a delicious flavour.

Serves 10

300 g beetroot, peeled and chopped (1 cup)

2 egg yolks

2 tbsp castor sugar

2 tbsp oil

1 tsp vanilla essence

150 g self-raising flour

1 tsp baking powder

1 tbsp cocoa powder

3 egg whites

Energy: 530 kJ/125 kCal
Fat: 5 g
Carbohydrate: 17 g
Fibre: 1.5 g

Beetroot is an excellent source of folate, which is important for the prevention of spina bifida in babies.

CONVENTIONAL

1 Preheat the oven to 180°C. Grease a 20 cm springform tin.
2 In a medium-sized saucepan simmer the beetroot in water over a medium heat until soft, then puree. Allow to cool.
3 In a mixing bowl beat the egg yolks and sugar together until creamy. Add the oil, vanilla and beetroot puree.
4 Sift in the flour, baking powder and cocoa.
5 In a separate mixing bowl whisk the egg whites until soft peaks form. Fold into the mixture.
6 Pour into the tin and bake for 40–45 minutes, or until a skewer inserted in the centre comes out clean.

MICROWAVE

1 Spray a 23 cm microwave-safe ring mould lightly with cooking oil.
2 Cut the beetroot into quarters, place in a round microwave-safe dish and cook on HIGH (100%) for 8 minutes, rotating the beetroot halfway during the cooking time. Cool slightly, then peel and puree.
3 In a mixing bowl beat the egg yolks and sugar together until creamy. Add the oil, vanilla and beetroot puree.
4 Sift in the flour, baking powder and cocoa.
5 In a separate mixing bowl whisk the egg whites until soft peaks form. Fold into the mixture.
6 Pour into the prepared mould and cook on HIGH (100%) for 5 minutes. Allo to stand until cold before turning out onto a wire rack. This cake is best eaten the same day it is made.

Baked Pumpkin & Honey Cheesecake

Pumpkin puree is a popular sweet pie filling in the USA and makes an equally delicious cheesecake.

Serve 10–12

300 g smooth ricotta (conventional method); 250 g smooth ricotta (microwave)

250 g light cream cheese

1 (55 g) egg

1 egg white

$^1/_4$ cup honey

400 g pumpkin, cooked and mashed (conventional method); 300 g pumpkin, cooked and mashed (microwave)

12 Granita biscuits, finely ground

2 tbsp water

nutmeg (microwave method only)

Energy: 605 kJ/145 kCal
Fat: 7 g
Carbohydrate: 15 g
Fibre: 0.5 g

Like most low-fat cheesecakes this is also a good source of calcium, phosphorous and riboflavin.

CONVENTIONAL

1 Preheat the oven to 180°C.
2 In a large mixing bowl combine both the cheeses, egg, egg white and honey. Add the pumpkin.
3 Pulverise the biscuits in a food processor. Add the water to the biscuits and mix. Press the ground biscuits into the base of a 22 cm springform pan.
4 Pour the pumpkin mixture over the top and bake until set, about 1 hour and 15 minutes.
5 Cool for 10 minutes before slicing.

MICROWAVE

1 Spray a 23 cm pyrex dish with oil.
2 In a large mixing bowl combine both the cheeses, egg, egg white and honey. Add the pumpkin.
3 Pulverise the biscuits in a food processor. Add the water to the biscuits and mix. Press the ground biscuits into the base of the dish.
4 Pour the pumpkin mixture over the top and cook on MEDIUM (50–60%) for 25–30 minutes, turning every 5 minutes. Allow cheesecake to rest for at least 30 minutes before serving. Sprinkle with nutmeg.

Hint

Pumpkin puree can be made quickly in the microwave. Pierce a small (500 g) butternut pumpkin six times, elevate it on a roasting rack and cook on HIGH (100%) for 10–12 minutes until soft. Scoop out the puree when the pumpkin is cool enough to handle. Use as a savoury or sweet pie filling.

Zucchini Cake

Zucchini are a slimmer's delight, having very few kilojoules and no fat. They are also versatile as they can be used in cakes, as well as savoury dishes and soups.

Serves 12

spray oil

2 zucchini, grated (for 2 cups)

2 tbsp lemon icing sugar

$^1/_2$ cup canola oil

$^1/_4$ cup prunes, roughly chopped

$^1/_4$ cup chopped pecans

$^3/_4$ cup All Bran cereal

2 (55 g) eggs, lightly beaten

$^3/_4$ cup self-raising flour, sifted

Energy: 685 kJ/165 kCal
Fat: 12 g
Carbohydrate: 11 g
Fibre: 3 g

Try giving fussy vegetable eaters their vegetables in a cake — don't tell them it's good for them!

CONVENTIONAL

1 Preheat the oven to 180°C. Spray a 20 cm cake tin with oil and line with baking paper.
2 In a large mixing bowl place the zucchini, sugar, oil, prunes, pecans, All Bran and eggs. Mix thoroughly with a wooden spoon.
3 Add the flour and mix until well combined.
4 Spoon the mixture into the tin. Bake for 40–45 minutes or until a skewer inserted in the centre comes out clean.

MICROWAVE

1 Spray a 23 cm microwave-safe ring mould lightly with cooking oil.
2 In a large mixing bowl place the zucchini, sugar, oil, prunes, pecans, All Bran and eggs. Mix thoroughly with a wooden spoon.
3 Add the flour and mix until well combined.
4 Spoon the mixture into the ring. Cook on MEDIUM HIGH (70–80%) for 8 minutes, elevated, turning halfway during the cooking time. Allow to stand for 4 minutes before turning out onto a wire rack to cool.

Hints

Here are other ways to use members of the pumpkin and squash family:

- *grate and use in place of carrot in a carrot cake*
- *slice and add to a tomato-based pasta sauce*
- *cut into strips and stir-fry*
- *steam briefly, halve, hollow, fill with cheese and fresh breadcrumbs, and bake until the topping is crunchy.*

Baby Lemon Cheesecakes

Snack-sized cakes are an ideal size for a manageable indulgence, as well as being convenient. It's a creative way of enjoying a controlled portion of a traditional cake.

Serves 6

250 g light cream cheese

1 tbsp castor sugar

$^{1}/_{2}$ cup light sour cream

zest of 2 lemons

$^{1}/_{4}$ cup fresh lemon juice

1$^{1}/_{2}$ tsp gelatine, dissolved in 2 tbsp hot water

6 Granita biscuits

Energy:	715 kJ/170 kCal
Fat:	12 g
Carbohydrate:	11 g
Fibre:	–

These calcium-rich cakes can be made even more nutritious by topping them with fresh blueberries or other seasonal fruit.

CONVENTIONAL

1 Line each cavity of a deep muffin pan with plastic wrap.
2 In a mixing bowl blend the cream cheese until smooth, then add the sugar, sour cream, lemon zest and lemon juice.
3 Add the gelatine to the mixture.
4 Pour into the prepared pan and top each cavity with a biscuit. Cover with foil.
5 Refrigerate for 2–3 hours or overnight.
6 Invert the pan to remove the cheesecakes.

Variations

Orange zest; coffee flavouring; any berries; peaches and apricots.

Hazelnut Chocolate Cheesecake

Cheesecakes are never out of fashion, and the variations are limitless. This makes a great hot-weather dessert — no oven necessary!

Serve 10–12

10 Granita biscuits, finely ground

2 tbsp water

2 (250 g) cartons light cream cheese

$^1/_2$ cup light sour cream

1 tbsp castor sugar

1 tbsp cocoa powder

3 tsp gelatine, dissolved in $^1/_4$ cup hot water

$^1/_4$ cup raisins

$^1/_4$ cup crushed hazelnuts

Energy: 830 kJ/200 kCal
Fat: 13 g
Carbohydrate: 13 g
Fibre: 1 g

A much lighter option than traditional chocolate cheesecake.

CONVENTIONAL

1 Lightly grease a 22 cm springform tin.
2 Mix the ground biscuits with the water in a bowl. Press the crumbs into the tin.
3 In a bowl beat the cream cheese and sour cream until smooth. Add the sugar, cocoa, gelatine and raisins. Sprinkle with the hazelnuts. Ensure the mixture is well combined.
4 Pour onto the biscuit base and refrigerate for 2–3 hours or overnight.

Variations

Try malt biscuits mixed with cinnamon or gingernut biscuits.

Orange & Honey Baked Cheesecake with Ginger Sauce

Ginger is a versatile flavouring, and can be used in sauces, jams, jellies, chutneys and confectionery. Golden ginger grown in Australia has a distinctive taste and flavour.

Serves 10–12

800 g smooth ricotta

$^1/_4$ cup honey

zest and juice of 1 orange

$^1/_4$ tsp vanilla essence

1 egg yolk

3 egg whites

1 tsp freshly grated ginger

250 g vanilla-flavoured low-fat yoghurt

Energy:	680 kJ/162 kCal
Fat:	7 g
Carbohydrate:	13 g
Fibre:	–

One serve of this cake provides the same amount of calcium as a glass of milk, so you can count it as one of your daily low-fat dairy serves!

CONVENTIONAL

1 Preheat the oven to 180°C. Lightly grease a 22 cm springform tin.
2 In a mixing bowl beat the ricotta until smooth. Add the honey, zest, juice, vanilla essence, egg yolk and whites.
3 Pour into the prepared pan and bake for 40–45 minutes. Cool for 10–20 minutes.
4 Mix the freshly grated ginger with the yoghurt and serve with the chilled cheesecake.

MICROWAVE

1 Spray a 23 cm pyrex dish with oil. Place a glass in the centre.
2 In a mixing bowl beat the ricotta until smooth. Add the honey, zest, juice, vanilla essence, egg yolk and whites.
3 Pour into the prepared dish and cook on MEDIUM (50–60%), elevated, for 30 minutes, giving the dish a quarter turn every 5 minutes. Stand for 30 minutes.
4 Mix the freshly grated ginger with the yoghurt and serve with the cheesecake.

Variation

Try a biscuit base for this cake to enhance the ginger flavour. Crush 12 gingersnap biscuits and mix with 2 tbsp oil. Press into the base of the springform pan. Bake for 6–7 minutes until the top is a golden to dark colour.

Hint

To prevent fresh ginger from browning after peeling, keep in cold water until needed.

Apple & Walnut Wrap

Granny Smith apples originated in Australia during the 1930s and are best for cooking as they have a tart flavour and crisp flesh.

Makes 1

spray oil

5 Granny Smith apples, peeled, cored and sliced

$3/4$ cup pitted prunes, roughly chopped

1 cup self-raising flour

1 tbsp brown sugar

1 tbsp margarine

50 ml light sour cream

50 ml skim milk

1 tsp cinnamon

1 tbsp ground walnuts

Energy:	600 kJ/145 kCal
Fat:	4 g
Carbohydrate:	26 g
Fibre:	3 g

A diet rich in a variety of fibre is important for good bowel health. This yummy dessert is loaded with fibre and is low in fat.

CONVENTIONAL

1 Preheat the oven to 180°C. Lightly oil a baking tray.

2 Place the apples in a medium-sized saucepan with a little spray oil and cook on medium heat until soft. This takes about 12–15 minutes. Drain off any excess liquid and allow to cool. When the mixture is cool, add the prunes.

3 Place the flour and sugar in a mixing bowl. Rub in the margarine. Mix together the sour cream and milk in a separate jug.

4 With a flat-bladed knife, mix in the milk and sour cream to form a dough.

5 On a floured bench, lightly knead and roll out the dough to 1.5 cm thickness.

6 Place the cooled apples with the prunes in the centre of the dough. Fold up the outside of the dough, leaving a small hole at the top. Brush with water and sprinkle with cinnamon and ground walnuts. Transfer to the tray, and bake in the oven for 35–40 minutes, or until the outside is golden brown.

Variation

Make individual desserts by dividing the dough into the desired amount of servings. Add 1 tbsp chopped nuts to the fruit mix.

Hints

- *The apples can be replaced with any type of stone fruit or pears.*
- *Apples can be cooked to a puree in their skins in the microwave oven in just 3–4 minutes. Place 4 in a microwave-safe container and microwave on HIGH (100%) for 7–8 minutes.*

Super Strudel with Apple, Raisins & Cinnamon

Serves 4

400 g apples, cored, peeled and cut into cubes

100 g Granita biscuits, finely ground

100 g raisins

1 tsp cinnamon

4 sheets filo pastry

extra cinnamon

spray oil

Energy:	1145 kJ/275 kCal
Fat:	5 g
Carbohydrate:	55 g
Fibre:	4 g

CONVENTIONAL/MICROWAVE

1 Preheat the oven to 180°C. Line a baking tray with baking paper.

2 Place the apples in a microwave-safe container and microwave on HIGH (100%) for 4 minutes to soften. Cool slightly, then add the biscuits, raisins and cinnamon.

3 To prepare the filo pastry sheets, sprinkle cinnamon between each of the sheets. Spray lightly with oil to help the pastry stick together.

4 Spread the mixture over two-thirds of the filo pastry and then roll up the pastry. Seal the ends with a little water and place the strudel, seam side down, on the baking tray.

5 Bake for 20 minutes until brown and crisp. Serve with **Ricotta Cream** (page 184).

Variations

- Use pears, peaches, quinces or plums.
- Sprinkle pastry sheets with finely ground walnuts.

New-fashioned Apple Pie

In Australia there are now 80 varieties of apples to choose from. Relatively low in sugar, apples such as Granny Smith cook up really well and fall to a puree, whereas higher-sugar apples like Pink Ladies keep their shape better during cooking.

Serves 8

Filling

400 g Pink Lady apples, peeled, cored and roughly chopped

1/2 cup water

1 tbsp castor sugar

3 tsp margarine (optional)

1 tbsp lemon juice

1 tbsp lemon zest

1/2 tsp cinnamon

1 tbsp brandy or brandy essence

1/2 tsp nutmeg

4 sheets filo pastry

2 Granny Smith apples, peeled and cored

lemon juice

1/2 tbsp castor sugar (optional)

Energy:	880 kJ/210 kCal
Fat:	7 g
Carbohydrate:	33 g
Fibre:	4 g

Filo pastry is a great low-fat substitute for the higher-fat shortcrust and puff pastries, especially if you don't add butter or margarine between each sheet.

CONVENTIONAL

1 For the filling, place the apples and water in a medium-sized saucepan and bring to the boil. Reduce the heat and simmer for 15 minutes, until the apples are soft but still hold their shape.

2 Place the cooked apples, sugar, margarine, lemon juice and zest, cinnamon, brandy and nutmeg in a food processor or blender and puree.

3 Remove from food processor and return to a saucepan. Cook the puree over a low heat, stirring frequently until a paste forms. Set aside to cool.

4 Preheat the oven to 190°C.

5 To make the pie, spray a 25 cm flan tin with oil and line with 4 sheets of filo. Fold down the edges to neaten.

6 Thinly slice the 2 apples and toss in lemon juice. Spread the cooled puree over the base of the pastry. Arrange the sliced apples on top of the puree. Sprinkle with castor sugar.

7 Bake for 20 minutes until golden brown and the apples are tender. Serve warm or cold.

MICROWAVE

1 To make the filling, place apples and water in a microwave-safe container and microwave on HIGH (100%) for 10 minutes.

2 Place cooked apples, castor sugar, butter, lemon juice and zest, cinnamon, brandy and nutmeg in a food processor or blender and puree.

3 Remove from food processor and return to a microwave-safe container. Microwave the apple puree on MEDIUM (50–60%) for 8–10 minutes, stirring every 2–3 minutes until a thick paste forms. Set aside to cool.

4 Preheat the oven to 190°C.

5 To make the pie, spray a 25 cm flan tin with oil and line with 4 sheets of filo. Fold the edges down to neaten.

6 Cut the 2 apples into thin slices and toss in lemon juice. Spread the cooled puree over the base of the pastry. Arrange the sliced apples on top of the puree. Sprinkle with the castor sugar.

7 Bake in the oven for 20 minutes until the top is golden brown and the apples are tender. Serve warm or cold.

Variations
Fresh peaches, apricots or pears could also be used.

Hints
- If you want the apples to break up, cook with a little water but no sugar. Apples release a good deal of their high water content when heated. Apple puree is also available canned.
- Serve with a dollop of **Apricot Sauce** (page 186) for a deliciously healthy dessert.

Pear Parcels

Serves 2

spray oil

2 pears

2 cups water

$1/2$ tsp allspice

1 stick cinnamon

1 vanilla pod

2 tbsp fruit medley

1 sheet filo pastry

Energy: 750 kJ/180 kCal
Fat: –
Carbohydrate: 43 g
Fibre: 6 g

Pears are a good low-glycaemic index fruit for keeping blood glucose levels under control.

CONVENTIONAL

1 Preheat the oven to 190°C. Lightly oil a baking tray.

2 Peel the pears and remove the cores from the base with a melon baller. Leave the stalk intact.

3 Place the pears, water, allspice, cinnamon and seeds from a split and scraped vanilla pod in a small saucepan. Bring to the boil, reduce the heat and simmer for 15–20 minutes until the pears are soft.

4 Allow the pears to cool. Drain and dry with paper towel. Place 1 tbsp fruit medley in the cavity of the pear.

5 Fold the filo pastry in half and cut in half. Place the pear on the pastry, round side of the pear facing upwards.

6 Gather the pastry sheet around the pear and tie with string. Place on a baking tray. Repeat with the other poached pear.

7 Bake for 10–15 minutes. Serve with **Custard** (page 182).

Variation

Use apples instead of pears, apricots or peaches.

Hint

The pears can be cooked in the microwave: place the pears, water, allspice, cinnamon and vanilla pod in a microwave-safe bowl and microwave the pear on one side for 3 minutes on HIGH (100%). Turn the pear over and microwave for a further 3 minutes on HIGH (100%).

Jam Leaves

Makes 12

3–4 sheets filo pastry

spray olive oil

honey or jam

Energy:	90 kJ/20 kCal
Fat:	–
Carbohydrate:	4 g
Fibre:	–

CONVENTIONAL

1 Preheat the oven to 200°C. Lightly spray a baking tray.
2 Spray the filo pastry lightly with oil. Fold the pastry in half and twist a couple of times. Tie at each end with string. Place on the baking tray.
3 Bake for 10 minutes. Cool, and remove the string.
4 Brush with hot honey or jam, and serve.

Hint

Pure olive spray oil is ideal for reducing the fat component when using filo pastry.

Sweet Pizza Amore

Serves 2

Energy: 935 kJ/225 kCal
Fat: 7 g
Carbohydrate: 37 g
Fibre: 4.5 g

Pecans are rich in monounsaturated fats and are used by astronauts in space as a low-fibre, concentrated energy source.

180 g peaches, fresh or canned

20 g chopped pecans

60 g prunes, pitted and roughly chopped

1 sheet filo pastry, folded in half and then cut in half

cinnamon

1 tbsp honey

CONVENTIONAL

1 Preheat the oven to 180°C. Grease and line a baking tray.
2 If using canned peaches, drain, reserving the juices. Dry the peaches. If using fresh peaches, wash and cut in half.
3 In a bowl mix together the peaches, pecans and prunes.
4 Sprinkle each sheet of filo with cinnamon.
5 Place the peach mixture in the centre of one piece of pastry and roll up. Tuck the excess under the fruit. Repeat with the remaining fruit and pastry.
6 Heat the honey in the microwave or place in a small saucepan and cook over a low heat for 2 minutes, and brush over the pizza.
7 Place on the baking tray and bake for 10 minutes. Serve hot or cold with **Custard** (page 182) or a dollop of vanilla-flavoured youghurt.

Hint

Use the juice of canned fruit to make a custard instead of milk.

PUDDINGS

PUDDINGS

PUDDINGS

What is the matter with Mary Jane?
It's lovely rice puddings for dinner again!

Puddings take us back to childhood, when grandmothers would turn out steamed bread-and-butter puddings from stale bread. The fillings were many and varied, such as peeled banana or apple tossed with spice or even chocolate morsels. Rum or brandy was added for special occasions.

The microwave oven is ideal for steamed puddings. The result is a moist texture somewhere between a cake and a pudding, while eliminating the traditional long steaming in a hot-water bath. Now they are no more time-consuming than any other dessert in your repertoire!

We hope you enjoy our South Pacific Rice Pudding, or Lime & Lemon Delicious, Cherry Clafoutis and other steamed puddings. The ultimate in comfort food!

Baked Lime & Lemon Delicious

Lime gives this pudding a fragrant and distinctive flavour. While it is closely related to the lemon, it is juicier, with a very sour pulp, which adds a new twist to an old favourite.

Energy: 422 kJ/101 kCal
Fat: 4 g
Carbohydrate: 12 g
Fibre: –

Serve this dessert with other fresh fruit to boost your daily fruit intake.

Serves 6

$^1/_4$ cup castor sugar

1 tbsp margarine, melted

2 (55 g) eggs, separated

2 tbsp self-raising flour

juice and zest of $^1/_2$ lime

juice and zest of $^1/_2$ lemon

1 cup low-fat milk

CONVENTIONAL

1 Preheat the oven to 180°C. Lightly oil a 20 cm pie plate.
2 In a bowl, beat the sugar and margarine until smooth. In a separate bowl, whisk the egg yolks well.
3 Add the flour, juice, zest, milk and egg yolks. Beat together well.
4 In a clean bowl whisk the egg whites until stiff peaks form. Fold into the citrus mixture.
5 Pour into the pie plate and set the plate in a roasting tray in the oven. Bake for 40–45 minutes until the filling is set and the top golden brown.

MICROWAVE

1 In a bowl, beat the sugar and margarine until smooth. In a separate bowl, whisk the egg yolks well.
2 Add the flour, juice, zest, milk and egg yolks. Beat together well.
3 In a clean bowl whisk the egg whites until stiff peaks form. Fold into the citrus mixture.
4 Pour into a medium-sized microwave-safe container.
5 Cover and cook on the edge of the turntable on MEDIUM HIGH (70–80%) for 5 minutes. Move the dish to the opposite side of the turntable halfway through the cooking time.
6 Allow to stand for 1–2 minutes to set. Serve warm or chilled.

Hints

- *Smell the lemons — American chemical science psychologists have found that the scent of lemon oil significantly improves people's mood.*
- *Place a lime in the microwave oven and zap on HIGH (100%) for 30 seconds to maximise the juice.*

Sticky Date Pudding

The fruit of the date palm is very sweet, ideal for those with a sweet tooth. The dates may be stuffed or dipped in melted chocolate for an occasional treat.

Serves 6

250 g dates, chopped

1^2/$_3$ cups hot tea

1 tbsp oil

1 (55 g) egg, lightly beaten

^{1}/$_2$ cup low-fat milk

1 tsp vanilla essence

2 cups self-raising flour, sifted

^{1}/$_4$ tsp baking powder, sifted

Energy:	670 kJ/160 kCal
Fat:	4 g
Carbohydrate:	29 g
Fibre:	4 g

This decadent dessert has nowhere near the fat of its traditional namesake, and provides you with plenty of fibre, calcium and iron.

CONVENTIONAL

1 Preheat the oven to 180°C. Grease and line a 25 cm × 15 cm loaf tin.
2 Place the dates, tea and oil in a small saucepan, bring to the boil, and simmer for 3–4 minutes. Remove from the heat and allow to cool.
3 In a mixing bowl combine the egg, milk and vanilla. Fold in the flour and baking powder. Stir in the cold date mixture. Ensure that all is well combined.
4 Pour into the prepared tin and bake for 35–40 minutes.

Hints

- *You can cook the dates in the microwave: place the dates, tea and oil in a medium-sized microwave-safe container, and microwave on HIGH (100%) for 2 minutes. Remove from the heat and allow to cool.*
- *Try adding some chopped dates to a sweet couscous for a Middle Eastern-type dessert.*

Cherry Clafoutis

This French dessert usually consists of black cherries arranged in a buttered dish and covered with a thick pancake batter. This is a lighter version, and is best served warm.

Energy: 310 kJ/75 kCal
Fat: 1 g
Carbohydrate: 11 g
Fibre: 1 g
Evaporated skim milk is an excellent source of calcium and can also be used in soups, pasta sauces, muffins and casseroles as an alternative to cream.

Serves 6–8

425 g can pitted cherries, well drained

1 cup light evaporated milk

1 tbsp sugar

2 (55 g) eggs

1 heaped tbsp self-raising flour

cinnamon for dusting

CONVENTIONAL

1 Preheat the oven to 180°C.
2 Lightly oil a 25 cm round pie plate, and arrange the cherries in the base of the dish.
3 In a bowl mix together the milk, sugar, eggs and flour to form a smooth batter.
4 Pour the batter over the cherries. Dust with cinnamon and bake for 45 minutes until the top is firm and golden. Serve hot or cold.

MICROWAVE

1 Arrange the cherries in the base of a medium-sized microwave-safe container.
2 In a bowl mix together the milk, sugar, eggs and flour to form a smooth batter. Pour the batter over the cherries.
3 Cover the container, elevate and place on the edge of the turntable. Cook on HIGH (100%) for 8–10 minutes. Move the dish to the opposite side of the turntable halfway through the cooking time.
4 Dust with cinnamon and allow to stand for 3 minutes before serving. This dish can be served hot or cold.

Variation

Morello cherries may be substituted for a tart flavour.

Hint

Turn the cherry juice into a sweet sauce by thickening with 2 tsp cornflour.

Summer Pudding

This pudding may be from humble origins, but served with ricotta cream, the result is a delight.

Serves 4

9 slices wholemeal bread, crusts removed

3 cups canned raspberries, redcurrants and strawberries

Ricotta Cream (page 184) flavoured with vanilla essence

CONVENTIONAL

1 With a rolling pin, flatten the bread. Line the base and sides of a 1 litre pudding basin with 6 slices of the bread. Ensure that the whole surface is well covered.
2 Mix the berries and some of the syrup in a bowl. Pour into the bread mould.
3 Cover the top with the remaining slices of bread. Cover with foil and place a weight on the top of the dish. Refrigerate for 12 hours.
4 Serve with **Ricotta Cream.**

Energy:	810 kJ/195 kCal
Fat:	2 g
Carbohydrate:	37 g
Fibre:	7 g

This refreshing dessert is loaded with dietary fibre and is incredibly simple to make.

Variation

Use gently stewed fresh berries if they are available, and serve with yoghurt.

Steamed Pineapple & Ginger Pudding

High in flavour and low in kilojoules, pineapple is a delicious tropical treat. These days it may be purchased fresh and peeled from most local supermarkets.

Serves 4

spray oil

100 g fresh pineapple, peeled and roughly chopped

1/2 cup self-raising flour

1/2 cup wholemeal self-raising flour

1 tsp ground ginger

40 g margarine, melted

1 tbsp brown sugar

1 tsp vanilla essence

1 (55 g) egg

1/4 cup skim milk

Energy: 640 kJ/155 kCal
Fat: 7 g
Carbohydrate: 19 g
Fibre: 2 g

CONVENTIONAL

1 Preheat the oven to 180°C. Lightly spray 4 custard cups (180 ml capacity) with oil.
2 Divide the pineapple between the cups.
3 In a mixing bowl sift both the flours with the ginger.
4 In a separate bowl, combine the margarine, brown sugar and vanilla. Add the egg and milk, stirring to mix thoroughly.
5 Pour the egg mixture into the dry mixture, combining well.
6 Pour 1/4 of the mix into each cup and place the cups in a baking tray that is half-filled with warm water.
7 Cover the tops tightly with foil, and steam for 25 minutes. Serve with **Custard** (page 182).

MICROWAVE

1 Lightly spray 4 custard cups (180 ml capacity) with oil.
2 Divide the pineapple between the cups.
3 In a mixing bowl sift both the flours with the ginger.
4 In a separate bowl, combine the margarine, brown sugar and vanilla. Stir into the flour.
5 Add the egg and milk and combine well.
6 Pour $1/4$ of the mix into each cup. Cover with plastic wrap and place the cups around the edge of the turntable. Cook on HIGH (100%) for 3 minutes, rotating cups halfway through the cooking time. Allow to stand for 1 minute. Serve with **Custard** (page 182).

Hint

To keep pineapple fresh, store in a cool place without too much variation in temperature. Constant changes in temperature can affect the flesh and cause black heart.

Crunchy Bread & No Butter Pudding

A new version of the tried-and-true favourite. Take advantage of the many varieties of bread now available to change the taste and texture.

Serves 6–8

8–10 slices wholemeal or mixed grain bread, with crusts

spray oil

1 tsp honey or marmalade

120 g mixed dried fruit, peaches and sultanas, large pieces roughly chopped

3 (55 g) eggs

1^1/$_2$ cups evaporated skim milk

1 cup skim milk

3 Granita biscuits, finely crushed

1 tsp nutmeg

Energy: 938 kJ/225 kCal
Fat: 4 g
Carbohydrate: 39 g
Fibre: 4 g

A few mouthfuls of this pudding will give you protein, carbohydrate, calcium, fibre and very little fat.

CONVENTIONAL

1 Preheat the oven to 180°C.
2 Cut the bread in half on the diagonal. Place half of the bread in a round 20 cm ovenproof basin that has been lightly sprayed with oil.
3 In a small saucepan heat the honey and dried fruits with water to cover on low heat until the fruit plumps up.
4 Whisk the eggs, evaporated milk and skim milk together.
5 Sprinkle half of the biscuits over the bread, then the fruit and honey. Layer the rest of the bread over the top. Sprinkle with the remaining biscuits.
6 Pour the egg and milk mixture over the top. Ensure that all the bread is covered with the milk. Dust with nutmeg.
7 Bake for 40–45 minutes.

MICROWAVE

1 Place the fruit in a microwave-safe container and cover with water. Cook on HIGH (100%) for 2 minutes. Drain the water, reserving the fruit. Drizzle the fruit with honey.

2 Cut the bread in half on the diagonal. Place half of the bread in a round 20 cm microwave-safe basin that has been lightly sprayed with oil.

3 Whisk the eggs, evaporated milk and skim milk together.

4 Sprinkle half of the biscuits over the bread, then the fruit and honey. Layer the rest of the bread over the top. Sprinkle with the remaining biscuits.

5 Pour the egg and milk mixture over the top. Ensure that all the bread is covered with the milk.

6 Cover, and cook, elevated, on MEDIUM (50–60%) for 20–25 minutes, rotating every 5 minutes. Dust with nutmeg, and allow to stand for 10 minutes before serving.

Variation

Dried fruits can be softened quickly in the microwave oven by covering with warm water and cooking on HIGH (100%) for 2 minutes.

Raspberry & Pear Sticky Pudding

Canned fruits offer a nutritious alternative to fresh fruits (choose those that have no added sugar) and can make a significant contribution to daily vitamin intakes.

Energy: 675 kJ/160 kCal
Fat: 1 g
Carbohydrate: 33 g
Fibre: 5 g

Raspberries are a very high-fibre fruit and also provide lots of vitamin C and iron. The frozen ones are a good alternative when fresh raspberries are not in season.

Serves 6

2 pears
$^1/_2$ cup apple juice
1 (425 g) can raspberries, drained syrup reserved
1 (55 g) egg, lightly beaten
$^1/_4$ cup castor sugar
1 tsp vanilla essence
$^3/_4$ cup self-raising flour
$^1/_4$ cup skim milk

CONVENTIONAL

1 Preheat the oven to 180°C. Lightly grease and line a 20 cm cake tin.
2 Peel and core the pears and cut into eighths (you should have 16 pieces). Place in a medium-sized saucepan. Add the apple juice and bring to the boil. Reduce the heat and simmer for 25–30 minutes until the pears are soft and most of the juice evaporated. Set aside to cool.
3 In a mixing bowl beat the egg and sugar together until light and fluffy. Add the vanilla, then fold in the flour and milk in alternate lots.
4 Fold in the pears and raspberries. Pour into the tin and bake for 20–25 minutes.
5 Cool slightly, and serve with **Custard** (page 182).

CONVENTIONAL/MICROWAVE

1 Preheat the oven to 180°C. Lightly grease and line a 20 cm cake tin.

2 Peel and core the pears and cut into eighths (you should have 16 pieces). Place in a microwave-safe container and add the apple juice. Cover with plastic wrap and microwave on HIGH (100%) for 8–10 minutes, stirring once or twice during the cooking proves. The pears should be soft. Drain the liquid and set aside to cool.

3 In a mixing bowl beat the egg and sugar together until light and fluffy. Add the vanilla, then fold in the flour and milk in alternate lots.

5 Fold in the pears and raspberries. Pour into the tin and bake for 20–25 minutes.

6 Cool slightly, and serve with **Custard** (page 182).

Variation

Any canned berries may be used in place of the raspberries.

Hints

* You can cook the pears in the microwave: place peeled and quartered pears in a microwave-safe container and add the raspberry syrup. Microwave on HIGH (100%) for 10 minutes, stirring once or twice during the cooking cycle. The pears should be soft and most of the juice evaporated. Set aside to cool.

* To warm canned fruits, place the fruit into a microwave-safe bowl with the juice, as this contains water-soluble vitamins and other nutrients.

South Pacific Rice Pudding

Coconut milk adds a distinctive and fragrant flavour to both sweet and savoury dishes. Coconut milk and cream are high in saturated fats, and so should be used sparingly.

Energy: 715 kJ/170 kCal
Fat: 2 g
Carbohydrate: 32 g
Fibre: 1.5 g

Basmati rice has a low glycaemic index, making it ideal for people with diabetes. It is useful for sportspeople before long events.

Serves 8–10

1 cup basmati rice

2^1/2 cups low-fat milk

1 tbsp coconut milk powder mixed with ^{1}/2 cup water or ^{1}/2 cup canned low-fat coconut milk

1 vanilla bean

1 tbsp finely grated lime zest

2 (55 g) eggs, separated

1 tbsp dark rum

2 tbsp brown sugar

420 g can tropical fruit salad, well drained

CONVENTIONAL

1 Preheat the oven to 180°C. Lightly grease a 23 cm ring tin.
2 Place the rice, milk, coconut powder, vanilla bean and zest in a large saucepan. Bring to the boil, then reduce the heat and simmer for 15–20 minutes.
3 Remove the pan from the heat and take out the vanilla bean. Allow to cool.
4 Stir the egg yolks, rum and sugar into the cooled mixture.
5 Place the egg whites in a bowl and whisk to soft peaks. Fold the cooled rice into the whites.
6 Spoon the mixture into the tin and place in a baking dish. Pour hot water into the baking dish to reach halfway up the tin. Bake for 35–40 minutes or until set. Allow to cool before turning out.
7 Fill the centre with tropical fruit salad.

MICROWAVE

1 Place the rice, milk, coconut powder, vanilla bean and zest in a large microwave-safe container.
2 Leave uncovered and cook on MEDIUM (50–60%) for 15–20 minutes until the rice is tender and the liquid has been absorbed.
3 Remove the vanilla bean and stir in the egg yolks, rum and brown sugar.
4 Place the egg whites in a bowl and whisk to soft peaks. Fold the cooled rice into the whites.
5 Line the base of a microwave-safe cake pan with paper towels and spoon in the rice mixture. Cover and cook, elevated, in the centre of the microwave oven for 4–5 minutes on HIGH (100%). Allow to stand for 4 minutes before turning out.
6 Fill the centre with tropical fruit salad.

Variations

Use canned mangoes or pineapples if preferred.

Hints

- *Lining the base of a microwave-safe oven cake container makes it easier to invert desserts and cakes onto a serving plate.*
- *Don't store limes in the fridge as this reduces, by up to half, the juice the limes will yield.*

Jam Puddings

New-fashioned comfort food, ideal for winter time.

Serves 4

spray oil

$2/3$ cup low-joule jam of your choice

$1/4$ cup castor sugar

1 (60 g) egg, lightly beaten

1 tsp vanilla essence

1 tbsp very hot water

$1/3$ cup self-raising flour, sifted

Energy: 745 kJ/180 kCal
Fat: 1 g
Carbohydrate: 40 g
Fibre: 1 g

Try these with a natural fruit spread as an alternative to jam.

Conventional

1 Preheat the oven to 150°C. Lightly spray 4 ramekins (125–180 ml capacity) with oil and spread the jam evenly over the base of each.
2 In a mixing bowl beat the sugar and egg for 2 minutes until pale and thick. Add the vanilla. Gently fold in the water and flour using a metal spoon.
3 Spoon the mixture into the prepared dishes.
4 Bake for 15 minutes or until golden and firm to the touch. Remove from the oven, run a knife around the edges to loosen and turn out the puddings onto a plate. Serve warm with **Custard** (page 182).

Microwave

1 Lightly spray 4 ramekins (125–150 ml capacity) with oil and spread the jam evenly over the base of each.
2 In a mixing bowl beat the sugar and egg for 2 minutes until pale and thick. Add the vanilla. Gently fold in the water and flour using a metal spoon.
3 Spoon the mixture into the prepared dishes.
4 Put the ramekins on the rim of the turntable at opposite sides to each other. Cook on MEDIUM HIGH (70–80%) for $2^1/_2$ minutes until just firm. Remove from the microwave, run a knife around the edges to loosen and turn out the puddings onto a plate. Serve warm with **Custard** (page 182).

Variation

You can add 1 tbsp cocoa with the flour.

Tangelo & Coconut Pudding

Tangelos are a cross between a grapefruit and a mandarine. Easy to peel with few or no seeds, they are bursting with juice, and add a zest to cakes, slices and puddings.

Serves 4–6

spray oil

15 g desiccated coconut (conventional method only)

2 (55 g) eggs, separated

60 g sugar

zest and juice of 4 tangelos (conventional method); zest and 200 ml tangelo juice (microwave)

40 g desiccated coconut (extra)

5 tbsp self-raising flour

½ cup skim milk

toasted desiccated coconut (extra; microwave method only)

Energy:	715 kJ/170 kCal
Fat:	6 g
Carbohydrate:	24 g
Fibre:	3 g

Tangelos are rich in fibre and vitamin C, and make a delicious alternative to oranges and mandarines.

CONVENTIONAL

1 Preheat the oven to 180°C. Spray a 20 cm square or round baking tin with olive oil and sprinkle with coconut.
2 In a mixing bowl beat the egg yolks and sugar together until thick and pale in colour. Add the tangelo juice and zest, and the extra coconut. Mix well.
3 Fold in the flour and add the milk.
4 In a clean mixing bowl beat the egg whites to soft peaks and fold into the flour mixture.
5 Pour into the prepared tin and cook for 40 minutes or until the top is golden in colour.

MICROWAVE

1 Spray a 23 cm microwave-safe ring mould with oil.
2 In a mixing bowl beat the egg yolks and sugar together until thick and pale in colour. Add the tangelo juice and zest, and the 40 g coconut. Mix well.
3 Fold in the flour and add the milk.
4 In a clean mixing bowl beat the egg whites to soft peaks and fold into the flour mixture.
5 Pour into the prepared mould and cook on MEDIUM HIGH (70–80%) for 8 minutes, rotating halfway during the cooking time. Allow to stand for 4 minutes before turning out onto a plate. Sprinkle with some toasted shredded coconut, and serve immediately.

Variation

Oranges may be used in place of tangelos.

Hints

- Add tangelo segments to salads.
- Tangelo segments are excellent palate refreshers and the zest adds zing to sauces, gravies and marinades.

Custard Apple Pudding

Custard apple is a fruit cultivated in the tropics. It is the size of a grapefruit with a rough green skin. The white flesh is juicy with a rose-like scent. Once the black seeds are removed it may be eaten with a spoon, or added to fruit salads and custards.

Energy: 635 kJ/152 kCal
Fat: 5 g
Carbohydrate: 18 g
Fibre: 2 g

Custard apples are an excellent source of vitamin C and fibre, and are low in kilojoules.

Serves 4

250 g ricotta

3/4 cup vanilla-flavoured low-fat yoghurt

1 (55 g) egg

2 tsp castor sugar

1 custard apple, peeled and cored

CONVENTIONAL

1 Preheat the oven to 180°C. Lightly grease 4 ramekins or soufflé dishes (100 ml capacity).
2 In a mixing bowl combine the ricotta, yoghurt, egg, sugar and custard apple. Blend with a stab mixer and beat well with a whisk to ensure a smooth finish.
3 Divide the mixture between the dishes. Place in a baking tray half-filled with water and bake for 25–30 minutes until the mixture has set. Do not cover the dishes.
4 Serve warm or cold with a kiwifruit sauce.

Fruity Banana & Strawberry Crumbles

Conjure up these crumbles in mere minutes, from the fruit in your fruit bowl.

Serves 2

1 banana, sliced

100 g strawberries, halved

200 g peaches, stones removed and sliced

Topping

1/2 cup rolled oats

1 tbsp coconut

1 tbsp honey

1 tsp orange zest

2 tbsp sultanas

Energy:	1245 kJ/300 kCal
Fat:	4 g
Carbohydrate:	60 g
Fibre:	7 g

Strawberries are an excellent source of folate, a vitamin that is important before and during pregnancy.

CONVENTIONAL

1 Preheat the oven to 180°C. Lightly oil 2 small soufflé dishes.
2 Stir together the fruits in a mixing bowl.
3 For the topping, combine all the ingredients in a separate mixing bowl.
4 Place half of the fruit mixture in one of the soufflé dishes and top with half of the topping mixture. Repeat with the second soufflé dish and the remaining ingredients.
5 Bake for 20 minutes or until the top is golden brown.

Variations

- You can use peaches, apricots and apples.
- Fresh or canned fruit can be used.
- Use untoasted natural muesli with the honey and orange zest in place of the oats, coconut and sultanas.

Apple & Blueberry Crumble

Blueberries are grown in nearly every state in Australia, so they come fresh from the farm throughout the warmer months. They are also available canned or frozen.

Serves 4–6

2 green apples, peeled, cored and sliced

1 pear, peeled, cored and sliced

250 g blueberries

2 tbsp lemon juice

2 tsp lemon zest

$1/4$ tsp cinnamon

$1/4$ tsp nutmeg

Topping

$1/2$ cup plain flour

$3/4$ cup rolled oats

1 tbsp brown sugar

1–2 tbsp margarine

$1/4$ cup pecans, chopped

$1/4$ cup desiccated
    coconut (optional)

Energy:	880 kJ/210 kCal
Fat:	7 g
Carbohydrate:	33 g
Fibre:	4 g

This is an excellent way to get fussy fruit eaters to include more nutritious fruits in their diet. There is the added bonus of fibre-rich oats and vitamin E from the nuts.

CONVENTIONAL

1 Preheat the oven to 180°C.

2 Place the apples, pears, blueberries, lemon juice and zest, cinnamon and nutmeg in a medium-sized saucepan and cook over medium heat until soft, approximately 20 minutes.

3 Transfer the cooked fruit to a 25 cm round ovenproof flan dish.

4 For the topping, in a mixing bowl combine the flour, oats and brown sugar. Rub in the margarine so that the mixture resembles breadcrumbs. Add the pecans and coconut and mix well.

5 Sprinkle the topping over the fruit and bake for 30 minutes or until the topping is golden.

MICROWAVE

1 Preheat the grill.
2 Place the apples, pears, blueberries, lemon juice and zest, cinnamon and nutmeg in a medium-sized microwave-safe container and cook on MEDIUM HIGH (70–80%) for 10 minutes.
3 For the topping, in a mixing bowl combine the flour, oats and brown sugar. Rub in the margarine so that the mixture resembles breadcrumbs. Add the pecans and coconut and mix well.
4 Transfer the cooked fruit to an ovenproof dish.
5 Sprinkle the topping over the fruit. Cook on HIGH (100%) for 5 minutes.
6 To brown the topping, place the crumble under the grill for 5 minutes.

Variation

Instead of blueberries use rhubarb, raspberries, plums, apricots, peaches or dried sultanas.

Hint

Use canned fruits of your choice for this dessert, and have them ready to go in the pantry.

SCONES & MUFFINS

SCONES &

MUFFINS

There is nothing like a homemade scone or muffin for a healthy snack. Once you have a good basic recipe, the variations are endless. Quick and easy to make, they are best eaten on the day they are made, but can be individually wrapped and frozen for a month. You will not have to forego them if you ensure that you keep freshly baked scones and muffins in your freezer ready for speedy microwave defrosting.

To defrost scones (30%):

1 scone — 15 seconds

2 scones — 20 seconds

3 scones — 35 seconds

4 scones — 45 seconds

Rewarming a scone takes just 10 seconds on HIGH (100%) in the microwave oven.

To reheat muffins, thaw at room temperature or DEFROST (30%) uncovered in the microwave oven on a roasting rack:

2 muffins — 45 seconds

4 muffins — 1 minute

6 muffins — $1^{1}/2$ minutes

To reheat in the oven, preheat the oven to 180°C, wrap the muffins in foil and cook for 10 minutes.

To reheat in the microwave oven, elevate on a roasting rack and microwave uncovered on MEDIUM HIGH (70–80%):

2 muffins — 45 seconds

4 muffins — 1 minute

6 muffins—$1^{1}/2$ minutes

Eat immediately.

Date Scones

Serve these scones with hulled and roughly chopped fresh strawberries and a spoonful of natural yoghurt. Or try honey yoghurt, fresh ricotta or frûche for a high-calcium, low-fat snack for between meals.

Makes 14–16

100 g dates, finely chopped

1/2 cup water

50 g margarine

3 cups self-raising flour

1 cup low-fat vanilla yoghurt

extra flour

Energy: 670 kJ/160 kCal
Fat: 3 g
Carbohydrate: 28 g
Fibre: 2 g

Variations

- To make pumpkin scones, use 1 cup light sour cream in place of the yoghurt and 100 g pumpkin puree in place of the dates.
- Try substituting fresh or frozen blueberries for the dates.

Hint

You can cook the dates in the microwave: place them in a small microwave-safe jug and microwave on HIGH (100%) for 4 minutes. Allow to cool.

CONVENTIONAL

1 Preheat the oven to 180°C. Line a non-stick baking tray with baking paper.
2 Place the dates and water in a small saucepan. Simmer over a low heat until soft.
3 In a large mixing bowl rub the margarine into the flour. Add the yoghurt and cooled dates and combine to form a dough. Lightly knead the dough and roll out to a thickness of 2 cm on a lightly floured board. Cut with a 5 cm scone cutter or knife, and place on a baking tray.
4 Bake for 12 minutes in the oven until the tops are golden brown.

Raisin, Bran & Cinnamon Scones

Packed with fibre, these scones are perfect for people with diabetes and for those wanting to keep regular and in shape.

Makes 12, or 6 large scones

60 g margarine

2 cups self-raising flour, sifted

2 cups unprocessed bran

1/2 cup skim milk powder

100 g raisins

1–2 cups water

extra flour

cinnamon powder for dusting

Energy:	860 kJ/205 kCal
Fat:	6 g
Carbohydrate:	31 g
Fibre:	7 g

CONVENTIONAL

1 Preheat the oven to 230°C. Line a non-stick baking tray with baking paper.

2 In a large mixing bowl rub the margarine into the flour, bran and skim milk powder.

3 Add the raisins and mix until combined. Add the water gradually to make a soft dough.

4 Lightly knead the dough and roll out on a lightly floured board to a thickness of 1–2 cm. Cut with a 6 cm scone cutter or knife and place on a baking tray.

5 Bake in the top shelf of the oven until the tops are golden brown, 10–15 minutes.

6 Dust with cinnamon, and serve for afternoon tea.

Bran Scones

*These are an old Scottish recipe. The title may sound bland but they are excellent for Sunday morning breakfast in bed. Try these scones with poached eggs and finely sliced prosciutto for a late breakfast or brunch, or with some homemade **Three-fruit Marmalade** (p. 171) for a touch of sweetness.*

Energy: 590 kJ/140 kCal
Fat: 5 g
Carbohydrate: 19 g
Fibre: 5 g

A rich source of insoluble fibre, important for a healthy gastrointestinal system.

Makes 12 small, or 6 large, breakfast scones

60 g margarine

2 cups self-raising flour, sifted

2 cups unprocessed bran

1/2 cup skim milk powder

1–2 cups water

extra flour

CONVENTIONAL

1 Preheat the oven to 230°C. Line a non-stick baking tray with baking paper.
2 In a large mixing bowl rub the margarine into the flour, bran and skim milk powder.
3 Add the water gradually to make a soft dough.
4 Lightly knead the dough and roll out to a thickness of 2 cm on a lightly floured board. Cut with a 4–5 cm scone cutter or a knife and place on a non-stick baking tray.
5 Bake in the top shelf of the oven until the tops are golden brown, 10–15 minutes.

Variations

Herb scones: As for **Bran Scones**, adding to the flour 1 tsp each of dried oregano, dried parsley and dried chives. If you use fresh herbs, increase each amount to 1 tbsp.

Wholemeal Scones

*These scones are similar to the **Bran Scones** (page 60); however, they are not as dense and filling to eat. Serve with creamy corn or baked beans with alfalfa sprouts for an excellent between-meals 'pick-me-up'. For a healthy alternative to jam and cream, serve with sweet fruit spread and whipped ricotta.*

Makes 14

2 cups self-raising flour

1 cup wholemeal self-raising flour

80 g chilled margarine

1¼ cups low-fat milk

extra flour

Energy:	512 kJ/122 kCal
Fat:	7 g
Carbohydrate:	12 g
Fibre:	2 g

CONVENTIONAL

1 Preheat the oven to 200°C. Line a non-stick baking tray with baking paper.
2 In a large mixing bowl mix the two flours together.
3 Cut the margarine into small cubes and rub into the flours until the mixture resembles breadcrumbs.
4 Add the milk gradually, and mix gently with a flat-bladed knife until the mixture almost comes together in a ball.
5 Lightly knead the dough and roll out on a lightly floured board to a thickness of 1–2 cm. Cut with a 6 cm scone cutter or knife and place on a baking tray.
6 Bake for 10 minutes or until the tops are golden brown.

Variation

To turn these scones into bruschetta, brush lightly with oil, toast and serve with slivers of mozzarella and roasted sweet red capsicums.

Hint

Add 2 tbsp of toasted seeds, or try sesame or pumpkin seeds, or pine nuts.

Cinnamon & Berry Muffins

A great coffee-time or afternoon treat. Any berry jam can be used — try one of the homemade jams on pages 171–8.

Makes 12 muffins

$^1/_2$ cup self-raising flour

$^1/_2$ cup wholemeal self-raising flour

2 tsp cinnamon

1 egg white, unbeaten

$^1/_3$ cup natural low-fat yoghurt

2 tsp vanilla essence

2 tbsp berry jam

2–3 tsp orange zest

olive oil spray

Energy: 250 kJ/60 kCal
Fat: 0.5 g
Carbohydrate: 12 g
Fibre: 1 g

CONVENTIONAL

1 Preheat the oven to 200°C. Lightly oil a muffin pan.
2 In a mixing bowl sift together the two flours and cinnamon.
3 In a clean mixing bowl mix together the egg white, yoghurt, vanilla, jam and zest.
4 Fold the flours into the wet mixture.
5 Spoon the mixture into the muffin pan and bake for 12 minutes or until the muffins spring back when lightly pressed. Remove the muffins, and cool on a wire rack.

Hints

- If you don't have a muffin pan, spoon the mixture into patty pans that have been placed in a shallow cake tin or baking pan. Use olive oil spray to lightly grease the muffin pan.
- Use fruit spread as a lower sugar option instead of jam.

Banana & Honey Muffins

This is a great way to use up overripe bananas for a mouthwatering snack. Serve while they are still warm with banana yoghurt.

Makes 11

¹/₂ cup self-raising flour

¹/₂ cup wholemeal self-raising flour

¹/₂ tsp bicarbonate of soda (microwave method only)

1 egg white

¹/₂ cup natural low-fat yoghurt

1 tbsp honey

2 large ripe bananas, mashed with a fork

cinnamon or chopped pecans (microwave method only)

Energy:	285 kJ/70 kCal
Fat:	–
Carbohydrate:	14 g
Fibre:	1.5 g

CONVENTIONAL

1 Preheat the oven to 180°C. Lightly oil a muffin pan.
2 In a large mixing bowl sift together the two flours.
3 Combine the egg white, yoghurt and honey. Add to the flours and stir well.
4 Add the bananas and mix until combined.
5 Spoon the mixture into the muffin pan.
6 Bake for 15–20 minutes or until golden brown. Repeat with the remaining mixture.

MICROWAVE

1 In a large mixing bowl sift together the flours and bicarbonate of soda.
2 Combine the egg white, yoghurt and honey, then add to the dry ingredients.
3 Add the mashed bananas and mix until combined. Spoon the mixture into a lightly greased microwave-safe muffin pan.
4 Place the muffin pan off the centre of the turntable and cook on HIGH (100%) for 90 seconds, then move the muffin pan to the other side of the turntable and cook for a further 60–90 seconds on HIGH (100%).
5 Remove from the pan when cool to the touch. Repeat with the remaining mixture. Sprinkle with cinnamon or nuts before serving.

Variation

Add 50 g chopped pecan nuts to the mixture.

Hint

Store in an airtight container for up to 1 day.

Apple Muffins

If you have teenagers in the house who are always hungry, they can feast and fill up on these low-fat muffins at any time of day!

Energy: 355 kJ/85 kCal
Fat: 0.5 g
Carbohydrate: 17 g
Fibre: 2 g

Snacking regularly on low-fat snacks is important for stabilising blood-sugar levels and for weight control.

Makes 8 large or 12–14 small muffins

2 medium-sized Granny Smith apples, peeled, cored and diced

$^1/_2$ cup self-raising flour

$^1/_2$ cup self-raising wholemeal flour

$^1/_2$ tsp bicarbonate of soda (microwave method only)

$^1/_2$ tsp cinnamon

1 tbsp honey

$^1/_3$ cup natural low-fat yoghurt

1 egg white, unbeaten

extra cinnamon (microwave method only)

CONVENTIONAL

1 Preheat the oven to 200°C. Lightly oil a muffin pan.
2 Cook the diced apple in a little water for about 10 minutes to soften. Allow the apples to cool.
3 In a mixing bowl sift together the two flours and cinnamon.
4 In a separate mixing bowl combine the honey, yoghurt and egg white. Add the cooled apples, combining well.
5 Stir in the dry ingredients. Mix until combined.
6 Spoon into a muffin pan and bake for 12–14 minutes or until the muffins spring back when lightly pressed. Remove the muffins and cool on a wire rack.

MICROWAVE

1 Place the apples in a small microwave-safe container and cook on HIGH (100%) for 4 minutes. Allow to cool.
2 In a mixing bowl sift together the two flours, bicarbonate of soda and cinnamon.
3 In a separate clean bowl combine the honey, yoghurt, egg white and the cooled cooked apples.
4 Add the flours and mix until well combined.
5 Spoon the mixture into a microwave-safe muffin pan.
6 Place the pan on the outside of the turntable and microwave on HIGH (100%) for 90 seconds, then move the pan to the opposite side of the turntable and microwave for a further 90 seconds on HIGH (100%).
7 Allow to cool and sprinkle with extra cinnamon to serve. Repeat with the remaining mixture.

Variation

Add $\frac{1}{3}$ cup sultanas.

Hint

If cooking in the microwave, remove the muffins from the pan when they are cool to the touch. This prevents a build-up of steam forming underneath and making the bottom of the muffin too moist.

Hazelnut Muffins

Hazelnuts give these muffins an enticing flavour. Try them as a warm dessert with low-fat vanilla icecream or as a mid-afternoon indulgence.

Makes 15

$^1/_2$ cup self-raising flour

$^3/_4$ cup self-raising wholemeal flour

$^1/_3$ cup natural low-fat yoghurt

1 egg white

2 tbsp Nutella

2 tsp orange zest

$^1/_2$ cup evaporated skim milk

$^1/_4$ cup chopped hazelnuts (microwave method only)

Energy: 310 kJ/75 kCal
Fat: 3 g
Carbohydrate: 9 g
Fibre: 1.5 g

CONVENTIONAL

1 Preheat the oven to 200°C. Lightly oil a muffin pan.
2 In a mixing bowl sift the two flours together.
3 In a clean mixing bowl combine the yoghurt, egg white, Nutella, zest and evaporated milk and add to the flour. Mix well to combine.
4 Spoon into the muffin pan and bake for 10 minutes or until the muffins spring back when lightly pressed. Remove the muffins, and cool on a wire rack.

MICROWAVE

1 In a mixing bowl sift the two flours together.
2 In a clean mixing bowl combine the yoghurt, egg white, Nutella, zest and evaporated milk and add to the flour. Mix well to combine.
3 Spoon the mixture into a lightly greased microwave-safe muffin pan. Sprinkle the top of each muffin with hazelnuts.
4 Elevate the muffin pan and cook on MEDIUM HIGH (70–80%) for 1 minute. Allow to stand for 1 minute. Repeat with the remaining mixture. Eat immediately, as the muffins toughen as they cool.

Variations

- Use tangelo or lemon zest instead of orange zest.
- Stir $^1/_4$ cup chopped hazelnuts through the mixture before baking. To serve, place one hazelnut on top of the muffin or dust with ground hazelnuts.

Golden Sweet Corn Muffins

Turn these golden muffins into a Mexican-style quick lunch by adding your favourite beans or salsa.

Makes 8

1¼ cups wholemeal self-raising flour

½ tsp bicarbonate of soda (microwave method only)

½–1 tsp sweet paprika

⅓ cup low-fat yoghurt

1 egg white

¼ cup low-fat milk (conventional method); ½ cup low-fat milk or evaporated milk (microwave)

2 tbsp freshly chopped chives

1 cup corn kernels, drained

extra paprika (microwave method only)

Energy:	400 kJ/95 kCal
Fat:	1 g
Carbohydrate:	17 g
Fibre:	3 g

These high-fibre muffins are great for breakfast on the run.

CONVENTIONAL

1 Preheat the oven to 200°C. Lightly oil a muffin pan.
2 In a mixing bowl sift together the flour and paprika.
3 In another mixing bowl combine the yoghurt, egg white, milk, chives and corn kernels. Add to the dry ingredients and stir well.
4 Spoon into a muffin pan.
5 Bake for 14–16 minutes or until the muffins spring back when lightly pressed. Remove the muffins and cool on a wire rack.

MICROWAVE

1 In a mixing bowl sift together the flour, bicarbonate of soda and paprika.
2 Combine the yoghurt, egg white, milk, chives and corn kernels and add to the dry ingredients. Mix until well combined.
3 Spoon into a microwave-safe muffin pan that has been lightly greased. Sprinkle with paprika.
4 Place the muffin pan on the outer edge of the turntable and cook on HIGH (100%) for 90 seconds; then move the pan to the other side of the turntable and cook for a further 90 seconds on HIGH (100%).
5 Allow to cool, then remove the muffins. Repeat with the remaining mixture.

Hint

Serve hot or cold with ricotta cheese and **Tomato Jam** *(page 175), or ricotta cheese and* **Chilli Ginger Jam** *(page 176).*

Sweet Potato, Polenta & Herb Muffins

These hearty muffins are ideal for brunch or a lunch box or picnic hamper. Try serving them at a barbecue in place of bread. You can vary the herbs used; fresh and dried work just as well.

Makes 10

$^1\!/_2$ cup wholemeal self-raising flour

$^1\!/_2$ cup self-raising flour

1 tsp bicarbonate of soda (microwave method only)

$^2\!/_3$ cup polenta

2 tbsp freshly chopped chives

2 tbsp freshly chopped parsley

1 (250 g) sweet potato, peeled and grated

1 egg white

1 cup evaporated milk or skim milk

paprika (microwave method only)

Energy: 510 kJ/120 kCal
Fat: 0.5 g
Carbohydrate: 24 g
Fibre: 2 g

CONVENTIONAL

1 Preheat the oven to 200°C. Lightly oil a muffin pan.
2 In a mixing bowl combine the two flours, polenta, chives, parsley and sweet potato.
3 Mix the egg white and evaporated milk together and add to the dry ingredients. Combine well and spoon into the muffin pan.
4 Bake for 15–20 minutes or until the muffins spring back when lightly pressed. Remove the muffins, and cool on a wire rack. Repeat with the rest of the mixture if necessary.

MICROWAVE

1 In a mixing bowl combine the two flours, bicarbonate of soda, polenta, chives, parsley and sweet potato.

2 Mix the egg white and evaporated milk together and add to the dry ingredients. Combine well, and spoon the mixture into a lightly greased microwave-safe muffin pan. Sprinkle with paprika.

3 Place the pan off the centre of the turntable and cook on HIGH (100%) for 90 seconds. Move the container to the other side of the turntable and cook for a further 90 seconds on HIGH (100%).

4 Remove the muffins from the pan to cool. Repeat with the rest of the mixture.

Hints

- *Serve with ricotta cheese, smoked salmon and yellow or cherry tomatoes.*
- *If using dried herbs reduce to 1 tsp each.*
- *Look for evaporated skim milk (Skinny Tinny) — it's a great source of the antioxidant vitamin A and calcium.*

BISCUITS

BISCUITS

BISCUITS

Every country has its own version of the basic combination of flour, butter and sugar. Being so versatile, biscuits can be carried almost anywhere, even during war (as was the case with Australia's Anzacs), and make handy snacks between meals or with a cuppa. Many, such as shortbread, also satisy the sense of tradition at Christmas and other festive occasions.

Biscuits are easier to make than many cakes, and take mere minutes to cook in a hot oven. They tend to last longer than cakes, and can be more easily eaten in smaller portions (except maybe chocolate and cream-filled varieties!) Once again, however, they are traditionally made with large amounts of butter or margarine to give a crisp mouthfeel and moist product.

We have developed a range of recipes that are low-fat alternatives to the classics, yet still quick, easy and absolutely delicious.

Almond Bread

This traditional Italian biscuit is perfect for a light snack with a cup of tea or after dinner. They keep well in an airtight container. Pecans may be used in place of the almonds if you like.

Energy: 210 kJ/50 kCal
Fat: 2 g
Carbohydrate: 7 g
Fibre: 0.5 g

The almonds provide vitamin E, and there is plenty of high-quality protein from the egg whites.

Makes 24 slices

3 egg whites

$^{1}/_{2}$ cup castor sugar

$^{1}/_{2}$ tsp vanilla essence (optional)

90 g plain flour

90 g whole almonds

CONVENTIONAL

1 Preheat the oven to 180°C. Lightly oil a small loaf tin.
2 Beat the egg whites until stiff. Gradually add the sugar and vanilla, if using, and continue beating until all is incorporated.
3 Fold in the flour and almonds.
4 Bake for 50–60 minutes.
5 Cool, wrap in foil, and allow to allow to stand for 3–4 days.
6 Slice the loaf very thinly with an electric knife. Place the slices on a baking try and dry out in an oven preheated to 150°C for 30 minutes.

Chocolate Biscuits

A delicious high-fibre, 'healthier fat' alternative for chocolate lovers to be enjoyed in moderation. Pack a few when you're going away or driving distances, to nibble with coffee.

Makes 25

1 cup (80 g) rolled oats

¹/₄ cup desiccated coconut

¹/₂ cup self-raising flour

¹/₂ cup wholemeal self-raising flour

50 g cocoa powder

¹/₂ cup sugar

1 tsp bicarbonate of soda

¹/₂ cup margarine

¹/₂ cup water

¹/₄ cup currants

¹/₄ cup peanuts

Energy:	425 kJ/100 kCal
Fat:	5 g
Carbohydrate:	11 g
Fibre:	1 g

CONVENTIONAL

1 Preheat the oven to 180°C. Lightly oil a baking tray.
2 Combine the rolled oats, coconut, both flours, cocoa, sugar and bicarbonate of soda in a large mixing bowl. Melt the margarine in a small saucepan and add to the dry ingredients. Add the water.
3 Add the currants and peanuts, and stir so they are well mixed through.
4 Roll the mixture into balls the size of 20-cent pieces. Place on the baking tray.
5 Bake in the oven for 15 minutes.

Bitter Chocolate Hedgehog

A good chocolate slice, served with coffee after a meal, is really satisfying.

Makes 24–30 slices

2 tbsp hot water

2 tbsp olive oil

2 tsp icing sugar

2 tbsp cocoa powder

$1/2$ cup orange juice

1 tsp vanilla essence

2 (55 g) eggs

1 cup plain flour

1 tsp baking powder

$1/2$ cup chopped pecans

$1/4$ cup sultanas

Energy: 635 kJ/150 kCal
Fat: 8 g
Carbohydrate: 17 g
Fibre: 1 g

This lower-fat version of hedgehog also has healthier fats from oil and nuts.

CONVENTIONAL

1 Preheat the oven to 180°C. Lightly oil a 20 cm square baking tin.
2 In a large mixing bowl mix the hot water, oil, sugar and cocoa to form a smooth paste. Add the orange juice, vanilla and eggs.
3 In a bowl sift together the flour and baking powder, and fold through the chocolate mixture. Add the pecans and sultanas, and mix until combined.
4 Pour the mixture into the tin and bake for 20 minutes.
5 Cool and cut into 4 cm cubes. Store in the refrigerator.

Cherry Ripe

The cherry season usually runs from November through to January, so enjoy them while you can. This slice is a lighter version of the traditional French cherry clafoutis.

Makes 20

1¹/₂ cups wholemeal self-raising flour

1 tsp bicarbonate of soda

¹/₂ tsp cocoa powder

2 (55 g) eggs

³/₄ cup castor sugar

2 tbsp oil

200 ml vanilla-flavoured low-fat yoghurt

¹/₂ cup cherries, fresh or canned, pitted

1 tbs dessicated coconut

Energy:	410 kJ/100 kCal
Fat:	3 g
Carbohydrate:	15 g
Fibre:	1 g

A lot less fat than the common chocolate bar, this is a great summer treat when fresh cherries are in season.

CONVENTIONAL

1 Preheat the oven to 180°C. Lightly grease a shallow 30 cm × 20 cm baking tin.
2 In a mixing bowl sift together the flour, bicarbonate of soda and cocoa.
3 Combine the eggs, sugar, oil and yoghurt in a food processor.
4 Add to the flours and stir until combined.
5 Spread the cherries into the tin and pour over the batter. Bake for 40 minutes.
6 Leave to cool in the tin before turning out.
7 Dust with coconut and cut into slices.

Variation

Plums maybe used as a substitute for cherries.

Hint

Cherries freeze successfully for out-of-season use.

Mango Meringues

A perfectly indulgent dessert that you don't need to save for very special occasions!

Makes 24

4 egg whites

¹/₂ cup castor sugar

3 blocks Vita Brits

¹/₂ cup chopped pecans

1 mango, peeled and stone discarded

1 tsp lemon zest

CONVENTIONAL

1 Preheat the oven to 160°C.
2 In a clean bowl whip the egg whites until stiff, and then gradually beat in the sugar.
3 In a food processor process the Vita Brits and pecans until finely ground. Fold into the meringue mixture.
4 Puree the mango and lemon zest, and fold into the mixture.
5 Spoon teaspoonfuls of the mixture onto a sheet of baking paper on a metal tray.
6 Bake for 30 minutes, or until lightly browned.

Energy: 150 kJ/35 kCal
Fat: 1 g
Carbohydrate: 6 g
Fibre: 0.5 g

Hint

Rub a lemon slice around the bowl before whisking the egg whites to get a better result.

Nutty Oat Crunchies

This is an updated version of an Aussie 'old timer', the Anzac biscuit.

Makes 16

$1/2$ cup crushed peanuts

$1^1/2$ cups quick oats

$1/2$ cup plain flour

$1/4$ tsp baking powder

$1^1/2$ tbsp brown sugar

2 tbsp oil

100 ml water

Energy:	380 kJ/90 kCal
Fat:	5 g
Carbohydrate:	10 g
Fibre:	1 g

A lower-fat version of traditional Anzacs, the oats in these biscuits provide soluble fibre and will suit many people with diabetes.

CONVENTIONAL

1 Preheat the oven to 180°C. Line a baking sheet with baking paper.
2 In a bowl combine the peanuts, oats, flour, baking powder and sugar.
3 Make a well in the centre and add the oil and water. Mix together until the mixture forms a dough.
4 Roll out the dough on a sheet of baking paper to 2 cm thickness. Cut out the biscuits using a 5 cm round cutter.
5 Place on the baking tray and bake until golden brown, 12–15 minutes.

Variation

Use pecan nuts for a change.

High-performance Sports Bar

For active people these dried fruit bars are a handy pick-me-up, especially after sport, so have them ready to go in your fridge. They are a cheaper alternative to commercial sports bars!

Per bar

Energy:	630 kJ/150 kCal
Fat:	5 g
Carbohydrate:	24 g
Fibre:	3 g

Meeting carbohydrate needs without excessive fat is important for active people, and these bars are portable, tasty and great for boosting energy levels for peak performance.

Makes 14 finger bars or 24 small cubes

1 cup dried sultanas (conventional method only)

1 cup fruit medley (microwave method only)

$1/2$ cup water (conventional method); 1 cup water (microwave)

$1/2$ cup chopped pecans

1 tbsp margarine

1 tbsp brown sugar (microwave method only)

1 tsp vanilla essence

1 (55 g) egg

1 tsp baking powder

1 cup quick oats

$1/2$ cup wholemeal self-raising flour

$1/4$ cup water (microwave method only)

1 tbsp runny honey or maple syrup

CONVENTIONAL

1 Place the sultanas and water in a small saucepan on a medium heat and simmer until the sultanas plump up. Add the pecans, and allow to cool.

2 Preheat the oven to 180°C. Lightly grease a slice tin.

3 Beat together the margarine, vanilla and egg. Add the baking powder and beat well. Add the oats and flour. Mix until all the dry ingredients are combined.

4 Stir in the cooled sultana and nut mixture. Add the honey.

5 Press into the tin and bake for 30 minutes, or until golden brown.

6 When cool, cut into long finger bars or small cubes.

MICROWAVE

1 Place the fruit medley and water in a microwave-safe container and cook on MEDIUM HIGH (70–80%) for 3 minutes. Add the pecans and allow to cool.

2 Beat together the margarine, sugar, vanilla and egg. Add the baking powder and beat well. Add the oats, flour and water. Mix until all the dry ingredients are combined.

3 Stir in half of the cooled fruit medley mix. Add the honey.

4 Press into a 1.5 litre microwave-safe container and spoon the remaining fruit mixture over the top. Microwave on MEDIUM (50–60%) for 5 minutes.

5 When cool, cut into long finger bars or small cubes.

CREAMY DESSERTS & ICES

CREAMY DESSERTS & ICES

Desserts can range from cooked fresh or dried fruits through to soufflés and custards, or sweet and indulgent treats.

Whatever your longing in fruit-based creamy desserts, warm or cold, our selection here takes no time at all to prepare. All are delectable endings to meals!

The fruit creams and custards are sure to be popular for sweet tooths of all ages.

The frozen desserts are not only cooling, refreshing and easy to make, they are a great way to make the most of the fruits of summer. Capture their aroma and sweet tang in granitas and sorbets, or in no-fuss desserts made from a combination of light sugar syrup, juice and fruit puree. No special equipment is needed, and the desserts store well in the freezer for several weeks.

Panna Cotta

This silky custard is an Italian classic, and originally made with double cream. Portions are always small because of the richness of the traditional ingredients. This lighter version can be served with a seasonal fruit puree.

Energy: 370 kJ/90 kCal
Fat: 0 g
Carbohydrate: 14 g
Fibre: –

This high-calcium, low-fat version of the popular 'cooked cream' dessert also provides useful amounts of the B vitamin, riboflavin, which is important for the healthy growth and repair of body tissue.

Serves 4

300 ml low-fat milk

1 vanilla bean or 1 tsp vanilla essence

1 tbsp castor sugar

$\frac{1}{2}$ cup hot water (conventional method); $\frac{1}{2}$ cup water (microwave)

3 tsp gelatine

200 ml vanilla-flavoured low-fat yoghurt

berries, for serving

CONVENTIONAL

1 Lightly oil 4 small ramekins.
2 In a small saucepan heat the milk with the vanilla and sugar until just boiling. Set aside.
3 Pour the hot water into a jug and gradually whisk in the gelatine until dissolved.
4 Strain the milk and remove the vanilla bean if using. Add the gelatine and whisk by hand. Add the yoghurt and whisk again.
5 Pour into the dishes and chill for 4–5 hours until set.
6 To serve, turn the creams out of the dishes by running a knife around the edges, or dip the dishes in hot water before unmoulding. Serve with berries.

MICROWAVE

1 Lightly oil 4 small ramekins.
2 Combine the milk, vanilla and sugar in a 1 litre microwave-safe jug. Cover the top with paper towels. Place the jug off-centre on a turntable in the microwave oven. Cook on HIGH (100%) for 2 minutes.
3 Combine the water and gelatine in a small microwave-safe jug. Dissolve on HIGH (100%) for 40–50 seconds.
4 Strain the milk and remove the vanilla bean if using. Add the gelatine and whisk by hand. Add the yoghurt and whisk again.
5 Pour into the dishes and chill for 4–5 hours until set.
6 To serve, turn the creams out of the dishes by running a knife around the edges, or dip the dishes in hot water before unmoulding. Serve with some berries.

Variation

Try serving with kiwifruit puree.

Hint

If vanilla bean is not available, use 1 tsp vanilla essence after the milk has been heated.

Roasted Peach Parfait with Yoghurt

Peaches are a sensuous fruit whether eaten fresh or poached, and served with a berry puree. Roasting lends an aromatic flavour to this parfait.

Energy: 290 kJ/70 kCal
Fat: –
Carbohydrate: 13 g
Fibre: 1 g

This parfait is high in protein and is a good source of calcium.

Serves 10–12

5–6 peaches, halved

$1/4$ cup castor sugar

$1/2$ cup water

3 egg whites

400 g vanilla-flavoured low-fat yoghurt

CONVENTIONAL

1 Preheat the oven to 180°C. Grease and line a 12.5 cm square baking dish with baking paper.
2 Place the peaches in the dish and bake for 40 minutes. Allow to cool.
3 Place the sugar and water in a small saucepan and stir over low heat until the sugar dissolves. Bring to the boil for about 5 minutes and remove from the heat. Allow to cool.
4 Beat the egg whites into firm peaks and fold through the yoghurt.
5 Fold in the cooled sugar syrup and pour into a shallow metal tray. Freeze until firm. When firm, place the mixture in a food processor and beat until smooth. Add half of the cooled roasted peaches and process further. Transfer the mixture to a round 20 cm cake container and refreeze until firm.
6 To serve, cut a wedge of the parfait and serve with the remaining roasted peaches.

Variation

Individual parfaits may be served in tall narrow glasses.

Apricot Cream

Apricots are at their best in January and February, so enjoy them raw at room temperature when the flavour is at its peak.

Serves 2–4

160 g apricots, halved and stones removed

1 tsp vanilla essence

1 banana

2 tbsp ricotta

50 ml evaporated milk or skim milk

100 g canned apricots with light juice

2 tsp gelatine

1 tbsp hot water

sprigs of mint to garnish

Energy:	710 kJ/170 kCal
Fat:	2 g
Carbohydrate:	30 g
Fibre:	4 g

Another calcium-rich dessert with a high-fibre, high-protein and useful iron content.

MICROWAVE

1 Place the apricots in 4 small custard cups or parfait dishes.
2 Combine all the ingredients in a bowl except the gelatine, water and mint. Mix well with a stab mixer.
3 Dissolve the gelatine in the water, place in a microwave-safe jug and microwave on MEDIUM (50–60%) for 30 seconds.
4 Add the dissolved gelatine to the milk mixture.
5 Quickly pour over the apricots and place the dishes, covered with plastic wrap, in the refrigerator. Chill overnight.
6 Serve with sprigs of mint.

Variation

Use the stone fruit of your choice.

Hint

Slice and serve a selection of fresh stone fruit as a tantalising fruit platter.

Blueberry Yoghurt Dessert

Blueberries are very popular and can be bought fresh, frozen or canned from most supermarkets.

Energy: 510 kJ/120 kCal
Fat: –
Carbohydrate: 20 g
Fibre: 1 g

Blueberries, like most berries, are an excellent source of vitamin C and provide fibre and some iron.

Serves 6–8

1 tbsp powdered gelatine

1/4 cup lemon juice

1/4 cup orange juice

1 tbsp honey

300 g fresh blueberries

500 g vanilla-flavoured low-fat yoghurt

2 egg whites

extra blueberries

CONVENTIONAL

1 Dissolve the gelatine in the citrus juices over medium heat in a small saucepan. Stir in the honey, and cool to room temperature.
2 Combine the blueberries and yoghurt, then add the gelatine mix.
3 Beat the egg whites until soft peaks form.
4 Fold through the yoghurt mixture.
5 Pour into a 2 litre icecream container and freeze until almost solid.
6 Transfer to the bowl of a food processor and process until smooth. This step is important, as it ensures no large ice crystals will form and ensures a smooth dessert at the end. Return to the freezer for 1–2 hours.
7 Serve with fresh blueberries.

Hint

Use blueberries in an all-berry fruit salad.

Passionfruit Custard Meringue

If you're lucky enough to have a productive passionfruit vine, freeze the fruit in its skin to use throughout the year. Alternatively passionfruit pulp is available in small cans in supermarkets.

Serves 10–12

5 egg whites

2 tbsp castor sugar

3 tsp custard powder

1¹/₂ tsp lemon juice

250 g vanilla-flavoured low-fat yoghurt

pulp from 6 passionfruit

CONVENTIONAL

1 Preheat the oven to 150°C. Line a baking tray with paper.
2 In a clean bowl whisk the egg whites together on high speed until fluffy.
3 Slowly add the sugar until the mixture is thick and glossy, then beat in the custard powder with the lemon juice.
4 Pile the meringue on the baking tray. Bake for 25 minutes until lightly coloured. Cool in the oven.
5 Mix the yoghurt and passionfruit together. Cut the meringue into squares and top with the mixture.

Energy:	210 kJ/50 kCal
Fat:	—
Carbohydrate:	8 g
Fibre:	2.5 g

Passionfruit pulp has lots of vitamin C and dietary fibre, plus loads of flavour in a small amount!

Variation

Pureed berries may be used in place of passionfruit.

Hint

Add passionfruit to **Ricotta Cream** (page 184) or jellies.

Strawberry Rhubarb Soufflé

While you may consider rhubarb a rather tart fruit, botanically it is a vegetable. It marries well with sweet juicy strawberries to make a tangy soufflé.

Energy: 270 kJ/65 kCal
Fat: 1 g
Carbohydrate: 5 g
Fibre: 2 g

You won't find many soufflés with as much fibre as this fresh dish. Rhubarb is high in calcium and iron, although these are not particularly well absorbed by our bodies.

Serves 6–8

150 g (4) sticks rhubarb, peeled and roughly chopped

$1/2$ cup water (conventional method); 1 tbsp water (microwave)

250 g strawberries, rinsed, hulled and roughly chopped

200 g light frûche

3 tsp gelatine

$1/4$ cup water (extra, microwave method only)

2 egg whites

1 tbsp castor sugar

CONVENTIONAL

1 Lightly grease 6–8 moulds (180 ml capacity).

2 Combine the rhubarb and $1/4$ cup of water in a medium-sized saucepan. Cook over medium heat for 10 minutes.

3 Stir in the strawberries and cook for a further 5 minutes.

4 Place in a bowl and refrigerate to cool. Fold in the frûche. Set aside.

5 Sprinkle gelatine over the remaining $1/4$ cup water in a small saucepan. Allow to stand for 3 minutes. Stir. Cook over low heat for 4–5 minutes until the gelatine dissolves. Cool.

6 In a clean bowl beat the egg whites with the sugar until soft peaks form. Reduce speed and gradually add the gelatine mixture.

7 Fold the egg whites into the fruit mixture. Spoon into the moulds and refrigerate until set.

MICROWAVE

1 Lightly grease 6–8 moulds (180 ml capacity).
2 Combine the rhubarb and 1 tbsp water in a 1 litre ovenproof jug. Cover with plastic wrap and cook for 3–4 minutes on HIGH (100%).
3 Stir in the strawberries, re-cover, and cook for a further 3–4 minutes on HIGH (100%).
4 Refrigerate to cool. Fold in the frûche. Set aside.
5 Sprinkle the gelatine over $1/4$ cup of water in a small microwave-safe jug. Allow to stand for 3 minutes. Cook on HIGH (100%) for 1 minute until the gelatine dissolves. Cool.
6 In a clean bowl beat the egg whites with the sugar until soft peaks form. Reduce the speed and gradually add the gelatine.
7 Fold the egg whites into the fruit mixture. Spoon into the moulds and refrigerate until set.

Hints

- Strawberries are available in a range of shapes and sizes. Remove the green stalk (hull) after washing and use in desserts, jams, sauces or simply eat fresh. They are available all year, are an excellent source of vitamin C, and low in kilojoules.
- If you use canned rhubarb, skip step 2 altogether.

Cherries & Lemon Ice

Serves 4

100 g plain low-fat yoghurt

200 g cherries, pips removed

$^1/_4$ cup lemon juice

1 tsp lemon zest

$^1/_4$ cup castor sugar

extra cherries

extra lemon zest

Energy: 410 kJ/100 kCal
Fat: –
Carbohydrate: 22 g
Fibre: 1 g

A great Christmas treat when sweet cherries are widely available.

CONVENTIONAL

1 Blend the yoghurt, cherries, lemon juice, zest and sugar in a blender until smooth.

2 Pour into a shallow cake tin and freeze until almost frozen. Break up roughly with a fork.

3 Transfer to a bowl and beat until smooth. Pour the mixture evenly into a 15–25 cm loaf tin and cover. Freeze again.

4 Transfer the tin to the fridge about 30 minutes before serving. To serve, invert onto a platter and garnish with fresh whole cherries and lemon zest. Alternatively, freeze the blended mixture in an icecream machine until thick and creamy. Store in a covered container.

Melon Granita Olé

I was introduced to this iced delight in Spain although it is Italian in origin. It is a half-frozen preparation, often flavoured with coffee or liqueur. Served in tall chilled glasses, topped with a lightly poached stone fruit, it makes a marvellous refreshment.

Serves 2

½ large melon or watermelon

1 tbsp icing sugar

1 tbsp lemon juice

1 tsp lemon zest

mint leaves

Energy:	190 kJ/50 kCal
Fat:	–
Carbohydrate:	10 g
Fibre:	–

It is important to drink plenty of fluids in warm weather, and this icy treat will help to boost your body's water levels in the nicest possible way.

CONVENTIONAL

1 Place all the ingredients except the mint leaves in a food processor and process until smooth.
2 Pour into a shallow metal tray. Freeze for 3 hours or until partially set.
3 Stir with a fork to break up ice crystals, and refreeze for 3–4 hours.
4 Spoon into glass dishes or drinking glasses and garnish with mint.

Citrus Granita

Energy: 280 kJ/65 kCal
Fat: –
Carbohydrate: 16 g
Fibre: –

A refreshing way to meet your vitamin needs with more than 3 times the recommended dietary intake of vitamin C in each serve.

Variations

Mango, peaches and strawberries, among many others.

Hint

Use more orange juice if you prefer it sweeter; grapefruit and lemon give a very refreshing tart flavour.

Serves 2

juice of lemon, orange and ruby red grapefruit to make 1 cup
(approximately 1 large fruit of each)
$1/2$ cup water
1 tbsp white sugar

CONVENTIONAL

1 Mix all the ingredients together and pour into a shallow dish.
2 Place in the freezer. Remove, and stir, every 30 minutes until slushy.
3 Serve in a tall glass.

Lemon Sorbet

Serves 4

¹/₄ cup sugar

1 cup water

3–4 lemons

7–8 mint leaves

Energy:	230 kJ/55 kCal
Fat:	–
Carbohydrate:	12 g
Fibre:	–

CONVENTIONAL

1 Combine the sugar and water in a small saucepan. Stir over medium heat until the sugar dissolves, and bring to the boil. Remove from the heat, and allow to cool to room temperature.

2 Juice the lemons to obtain 200 ml of juice. Strain. Add the juice to the cooled syrup.

3 Pour the lemon syrup into the metal tray, cover with foil, and place in the freezer. Freeze for 3–4 hours.

4 Remove from the freezer and place in the food processor. Add the mint leaves and process until smooth.

5 Transfer to an airtight container and freeze for a further 2–3 hours. The sorbet can be eaten without the mint if preferred. However, it may need to be diluted slightly, due to the lower sugar content.

CHEATING

with

Chocolate

CHEATING *with* CHOCOLATE

Most people crave for a chocolate fix from time to time; however, if any food is associated with guilt, it has to be chocolate, probably because 50 per cent of the energy in chocolate comes from fat! There are a number of ways to get your chocolate hit without being run over by the kilojoules and fat, and we have incorporated many into the following recipes.

- Use chocolate to drizzle on biscuits and cakes, or as a coating on fruit or half-cookies. This creates an attractive finish using a minimum of chocolate.
- When a recipe calls for chopped chocolate, reduce the suggested amount by $1/3$–$1/2$.
- Include a few chocolate chips in a low-fat muffin or biscuit recipe for a hint of chocolate without overload.
- Dust cakes with a light mix of cocoa powder and icing sugar.
- Cocoa powder is relatively low in fat, and can be used for delicious low-fat chocolate cakes and desserts if used in recipes with low-fat ingredients such as skim milk, light cream cheese, ricotta, etc.
- Make a low-fat chocolate custard with a little drinking chocolate added to your regular low-fat custard.
- Combine a low-fat chocolate icecream with pears or strawberries for a simple dessert.
- Low-fat chocolate icecream blended with banana and low-fat milk makes a refreshing smoothie.
- Fill meringue shells with light chocolate mousse, and top with loads of fresh berries.

101

Basic Chocolate Cake

A versatile chocolate cake that can be turned into a Black Forest cake with the addition of ricotta cream and canned cherries.

Energy: 360 kJ/86 kCal
Fat: 1 g
Carbohydrate: 17 g
Fibre: 1 g

This low-fat chocolate cake can be made even more delicious by topping it with fresh tropical fruit dusted with icing sugar.

Serves 14–16

1 cup self-raising flour

$^1/_2$ cup wholemeal self-raising flour

1 tsp bicarbonate of soda

$^1/_2$ cup castor sugar

3 tbsp cocoa powder

1 cup water

5 tbsp oil

1 tbsp balsamic vinegar

1 tsp vanilla essence

CONVENTIONAL

1 Preheat the oven to 180°C. Lightly grease and line a 16 cm square cake tin.
2 Sift the dry ingredients together into a mixing bowl.
3 Add the water, oil, vinegar and vanilla, and stir well to form a smooth batter.
4 Pour the cake mix into the tin and bake for 25 minutes.
5 Allow to stand for 5 minutes before turning out on the rack to cool.

MICROWAVE

1 Line the base of a microwave-safe cake pan with absorbent paper towels.
2 Sift the dry ingredients together into a mixing bowl.
3 Add the water, oil, vinegar and vanilla, and stir well to form a smooth batter.
4 Spoon the cake mixture into the pan and spread evenly.
5 Cover with paper towels and cook, elevated, in the centre of the microwave oven on HIGH (100%) for 4 minutes.
6 Allow to stand, still covered with paper towel, for 10 minutes before turning out onto the rack to cool.

Toppings and serving suggestions

- Melt a small amount of chocolate (about 1 tbsp). Pour into the corner of a plastic bag. Snip the end and drizzle over the cake.
- Mix 1 tbsp cocoa powder, 1 tsp icing sugar and 2 tbsp water together to form a paste. Pour into the corner of a plastic bag. Snip the end and drizzle over the cake.
- Mix together smooth ricotta, and canned blueberries or raspberries with some of the juice and 1 tsp vanilla essence.
- Lemon, lime or orange zest also adds an attractive flavour to ricotta.
- Fresh strawberries with 1 tsp icing sugar sprinkled over the top looks fantastic and adds a tart flavour to the cake.

Hints

- *Leave the batter to stand for 10 minutes before cooking in the microwave to ensure an evenly cooked cake.*
- *Balsamic vinegar is naturally sweeter than other vinegars. It is also a low-sodium seasoning. Try sprinkling it over fresh strawberries to highlight their flavour.*

Chocolate Orange Roll

Serves 10

Sponge

2 egg whites

2 tbsp castor sugar

2 (55 g) eggs

2 tbsp cornflour mixed with 1 tbsp cocoa powder

extra cocoa powder

Filling

100 g ricotta

1 egg white

100 g low-fat yoghurt

1 tsp vanilla essence

1 tsp castor sugar

zest of 1 orange

Energy: 400 kJ/95 kCal
Fat: 5 g
Carbohydrate: 6 g
Fibre: –

This low-fat treat is packed with high-quality protein for muscle growth and repair, and other important functions in the body.

CONVENTIONAL

1 Preheat the oven to 200°C. Grease and line a 25–30 cm baking sheet.
2 To make the sponge, in a bowl, whip the egg whites with 1 tbsp sugar until stiff peaks form.
3 In a separate bowl, whip the eggs until they are pale and thick.
4 Fold the cornflour mixture into the egg mixture, then gently fold the egg whites through.
5 Spread the mixture onto the baking sheet and bake for 10 minutes. Cool with a tea towel wrapped over the top.
6 To make the filling, in a bowl beat the ricotta and egg white until smooth.
7 Add the yoghurt, vanilla, sugar and zest. Mix until smooth, then refrigerate.
8 To assemble, spread two-thirds of the filling over the cooled cake. Roll up and dust with cocoa powder. Serve chilled.

Variation

Mix berries through the yoghurt mix and garnish with more fruit.

Chocolate Polenta Cake

The addition of polenta gives this chocolate cake a firmer texture, which makes a small slice a substantial serving.

Makes 14–16 slices

1 tbsp cocoa powder

¹/₄ cup water

250 g dark chocolate, broken into pieces

2 (55 g) eggs

¹/₂ cup castor sugar

90 g fine polenta

¹/₄ cup marsala

4 egg whites

1 punnet strawberries, roughly chopped

1 tsp icing sugar

Energy:	540 kJ/130 kCal
Fat:	5 g
Carbohydrate:	20 g
Fibre:	–

If you keep the slices of this cake small, you can enjoy chocolate without excessive fat.

CONVENTIONAL

1 Preheat the oven to 180°C. Lightly grease and flour a 20 cm springform pan.
2 Mix the cocoa and water to form a thick paste.
3 Melt the chocolate in a small saucepan over medium heat, stirring continuously. Stir the cocoa paste into the chocolate.
4 In a mixing bowl beat the eggs with ¹/₄ cup of the sugar until light and fluffy.
5 Fold in the chocolate mix. Add the polenta and marsala.
6 In a clean mixing bowl beat the egg whites until soft peaks form, then add the rest of the sugar (¹/₄ cup) and beat until stiff and glossy. Fold into the mixture.
7 Pour the mixture into the pan and bake for 40 minutes. The cake will sink as it cools.
8 To serve, remove the cake from the tin, and scatter the strawberries over the top. Sieve icing sugar over the top.

Chocolate Tiramisu

Tiramisu means 'pick-me-up' and is usually made with mascarpone and sponge fingers. This low-fat version is just as flavoursome.

Serves 10

Sponge

2 egg whites

2 tbsp castor sugar

2 (55 g) eggs

2 tbsp cornflour

Custard

3 tbsp custard powder

1 cup skim milk

2 tbsp castor sugar

2 tsp vanilla essence

2 egg whites

130 g ricotta

130 g low-fat yoghurt

1¹/₂ tsp strong coffee

1 cup hot water

2 tbsp marsala

1 tbsp cocoa powder

Energy: 425 kJ/100 kCal
Fat: 3 g
Carbohydrate: 13 g
Fibre: –

CONVENTIONAL

1 Preheat the oven to 200°C. Grease and line a 16 cm cake tin.
2 To make the sponge, in a mixing bowl, whip the egg whites with 1 tbsp sugar until stiff peaks form.
3 In a separate mixing bowl whip the eggs with the remaining sugar until pale and thick. Fold in the cornflour, and gently fold through the egg whites.
4 Spread into the tin and bake for 10 minutes until lightly browned. Allow to cool.
5 To make the custard, stir the custard powder and 2 tbsp of milk until dissolved in a small saucepan. Add the remaining milk, sugar and vanilla. Heat the saucepan over medium

heat until the custard begins to thicken. Remove from the heat and allow to cool.

6 In a mixing bowl beat the egg whites until soft peaks form.

7 In a separate mixing bowl beat the ricotta and yoghurt together until smooth. Add the cooled custard and beat until the mixture is smooth. Fold in the egg whites.

8 To assemble, cut the cooled sponge into finger lengths (around 10 fingers). Mix the coffee and hot water, and stir until dissolved. Add the marsala.

9 Dip the sponge fingers lightly into the coffee mixture, then place in the base of a loaf tin. Cover with the custard mixture and dust with cocoa powder. Repeat with the remaining sponge fingers. Chill for 5–6 hours before serving.

MICROWAVE

1 Preheat the oven to 200°C. Grease and line a 16 cm cake tin.

2 In a mixing bowl whip the egg whites with 1 tbsp sugar until stiff peaks form.

3 In a separate mixing bowl whip the eggs with the remaining sugar until pale and thick. Fold in the cornflour, and then gently fold through the egg whites.

4 Spread into the tin and bake for 10 minutes until lightly browned. Allow to cool.

5 To make the custard, stir the custard powder and 2 tbsp of milk until dissolved in a microwave-safe jug. Add the remaining milk, sugar and vanilla. Heat in the microwave for 90 seconds on HIGH (100%) or until the custard begins to thicken. Allow to cool.

6 In a mixing bowl beat the egg whites until stiff peaks form.

7 In a separate mixing bowl beat the ricotta and yoghurt together until smooth. Add the cooled custard and beat until the mixture is smooth. Fold in the egg whites.

8 To assemble, cut the cooled sponge into finger lengths (around 10 fingers). Mix the coffee and hot water, and stir until dissolved. Add the marsala.

9 Dip the sponge fingers into the coffee mixture, then place in the base of a loaf tin. Cover with the custard mixture and dust with cocoa. Repeat with the other fingers. Chill for 5–6 hours before serving.

Variations

Rum or brandy may be used in place of marsala.

Hint

This dessert can be made in individual containers to achieve portion control.

Chocolate Soufflé

One of the great French classic dishes that is always an irresistible treat at the end of a meal. This soufflé is foolproof if you weigh the ingredients and follow the procedure exactly. 'Bonne chance!'

Serves 8

1 tbsp chocolate chips

1 tbsp cocoa powder

2 tbsp water

3/4 cup vanilla-flavoured low-fat yoghurt

1/4 cup light sour cream

2 (55 g) eggs

1 tbsp sugar

1/4 cup self-raising flour

1 tbsp marsala

3 egg whites

Energy: 430 kJ/100 kCal

Fat: 4 g

Carbohydrate: 11 g

Fibre: –

A light and healthy soufflé, great for chocoholics who are trying to keep their body fat under control.

CONVENTIONAL/MICROWAVE

1 Preheat the oven to 180°C. Lightly grease 8 1-cup capacity soufflé dishes.

2 In a microwave-safe jug place the chocolate chips, cocoa and water, and cook for 1 minute on MEDIUM (50%).

3 Place the yoghurt and sour cream in a bowl and cook for 1 minute on MEDIUM (50%). Leave the mixes separate, do not combine at this point. (See Hint.)

4 In a medium-sized container beat the eggs and sugar together until pale and thick. Gradually beat in the flour and then add the yoghurt mix, stirring well. Cook for 1 minute on MEDIUM (50%) to thicken the mixture.

5 Add the chocolate mixture and the marsala. Stir until well combined.

6 In a clean bowl whisk the egg whites until soft peaks form. Fold into the chocolate mixture.

7 Spoon into the soufflé dishes and bake for 25 minutes until puffed.

8 Serve with fruit syrup, sauce or **Custard** (page 182).

Hints

- *The key to a good soufflé is to hand-beat the egg whites to create a smooth texture.*

- *To melt chocolate conventionally, place the chocolate pieces with the cocoa powder, water and half the yoghurt in a heatproof bowl over a saucepan of simmering water, stirring constantly.*

Chocolate Mousse with Blueberry Garnish

Blueberries not only taste good, they are low in kilojoules as well as being nutritious. If buying them fresh look for those that are large, plump and uniform in size.

Serves 6

250 g smooth ricotta

$1/4$ cup castor sugar

2 tbsp cocoa powder, sifted

$1/2$ tsp orange brandy essence

3 egg whites

Garnish

1 (425 g) can blueberries in syrup, drained

1 tsp orange brandy essence

2 tsp orange zest

Energy:	695 kJ/165 kCal
Fat:	5 g
Carbohydrate:	21 g
Fibre:	3 g

The ricotta in this mousse makes it a calcium and protein-rich dessert and the cocoa provides valuable amounts of iron.

CONVENTIONAL

1 In a bowl and with a hand beater, mix the ricotta, sugar, cocoa and essence together until smooth.
2 In a clean bowl beat the egg whites until firm peaks stage. Fold into the chocolate mixture.
3 Spoon the mousse into individual serving dishes and refrigerate for 1 hour until firm.
4 For the garnish, combine the berries and essence. Refrigerate until ready to serve.
5 To serve, spoon the blueberries over the top of the mousse and decorate with the orange rind.

Variation

These berries can also be used as a puree.

Hint

Wash fresh blueberries only just before use. They store refrigerated for up to two weeks.

Chocolate-tipped Fruit

Chocolate-tipped fruit is a great alternative to dessert; ideal for nibbling on after dinner with coffee.

Each piece of fruit

Energy:	110 kJ/26 kCal
Fat:	1 g
Carbohydrate:	3 g
Fibre:	–

While these are a delicious way to enjoy fruit for dessert, keep in mind that few people stop at one or two — they are very moreish!

Serves 2–4

100 g chocolate

200 g strawberries

1 banana

1 kiwifruit

4 dates

CONVENTIONAL

1 Place the chocolate in the top of a double boiler and set over hot water. The chocolate will take 10–12 minutes to melt.
2 Prepare the fruit: wash the strawberries; cut the banana into 2 cm lengths; and peel the kiwifruit and cut into quarters.
3 With a teaspoon place a small portion of chocolate onto one end of each piece of fruit. Allow to dry and serve.

MICROWAVE

1 In a microwave-safe jug melt the chocolate for 4–5 minutes on MEDIUM (50%).
2 Prepare the fruit: wash the strawberries; cut the banana into 2 cm lengths; and peel the kiwifruit and cut into quarters.
3 With a teaspoon place a small portion of chocolate onto one end of each piece of fruit. Allow to dry and serve.

Hint

If the kiwifruit are firm, ripen them by placing in your fruit bowl with apples or bananas. Once they are ripe, keep them in your refrigerator.

Special Occasion Chocolates

These melt-in-your-mouth chocolates are ideal for a moment of decadent pleasure at Easter or on your birthday. Ensure that you stop at one or two!

Makes 36–40

400 g quality cooking chocolate, broken into squares

8 tbsp finely chopped dried fruit salad

2 tbsp flaked almonds

MICROWAVE

1 Cover 3 baking trays with baking paper.
2 Place the chocolate in a medium-sized microwave ovenproof glass jug and cook on MEDIUM (50%) for 4–5 minutes (the chocolate should still be glossy). Stir the chocolate.
3 Drop teaspoonfuls of chocolate onto the prepared trays, leaving room for it to spread (about 4 cm).
4 Working quickly, drop $^1/2$ tsp of dried fruit and a flaked almond on each chocolate. When all are assembled, refrigerate to set.
5 To store remove the chocolate with a spatula and store in an airtight container in a cool place for up to one week.

Each 5 g serve

Energy: 95 kJ/25 kCal
Fat: 1 g
Carbohydrate: 3 g
Fibre: –

These fit under the indulgence category of healthy eating. Enjoy them as a treat with a good glass of bubbly and some special company.

Variations

Use dried fruit of your choice for the topping.

Hints

- *Chocolate pieces melt more efficiently in the microwave oven.*
- *Chocolate can also be melted on the stove. Place the chocolate in the top of a double boiler and place over hot water. It will take 10–12 minutes to melt.*

FRUITS

FRUITS

Cherries Best eaten fresh, they can also be added to baked dishes such as clafoutis and strudels. Freeze them to enjoy in winter.

Figs Serve with a wedge of fresh ricotta and pecan nuts, or turn into fig jam.

Grapefruit Add to a mixed lettuce salad or warm under the grill for an easy entrée.

Grapes Freeze in the summer for an icy treat or add them to jellies.

Kiwifruit Slice as part of a layered fruit salad, or cut the top off and eat with a spoon for a low-kilojoule snack.

Loganberries Eat fresh, or use in desserts and jam.

Mandarines Easy to peel and eat. Make a warm mandarine fruit salad or add to a Mediterranean-style salad.

Nashi A popular Asian fruit best eaten raw. Serve segments in salads or alongside white meat or shellfish.

Oranges Juice for a thirst quencher, or make marmalade, or use as a glaze for pork chops and poultry.

Pawpaw   Eat raw with a squeeze of lime juice for breakfast, or slice into a stir-fry if they are green.

Quinces   Microwave thin slices with fruit juice and honey, or add to other fruits when making jam as they are high in pectin.

Raspberries   Eat fresh with yoghurt, or turn into a sauce or jam.

Pineapples   Stir-fry with prawns and ginger or add to beef kebabs. Barbecue slices to go with meat and poultry.

Strawberries   Ideal as snacks, in dips, drinks or desserts. Make a salsa with red onion and mint, and serve with smoked trout or avocado halves.

Tamarillo   Poach them or slice and stew with fruit juice.

Watermelon   Buy the seedless variety and make granita; add to a melon salad; or eat raw as a thirst quencher.

Juices   Freeze tetrapacks of juice: they'll thaw nicely for lunch at the office or school.

Poached Pears with Passionfruit

The ever-available pear is an ideal food for busy people because it provides energy-giving carbohydrates in a portable form. It can be poached in fruit juice or wine. Pears look very enticing when served with assorted fresh or dried fruit, or low-fat cheese.

Energy:	830 kJ/200 kCal
Fat:	0.5 g
Carbohydrate:	37 g
Fibre:	7 g

Passionfruit is rich in fibre due to the small, edible seeds. Like most fruits, it is a valuable source of vitamin C.

Serves 2

$^1/_2$ cup water (conventional method only)

2 pears, peeled, cored and sliced

1 tbsp runny honey

2 passionfruit

1 cup plain low-fat yoghurt

CONVENTIONAL

1 Place the water in a small saucepan and bring to the boil. Add the pears and honey, and reduce the heat. Simmer for 10 minutes.
2 Allow the pears to cool slightly. Mix the passionfruit and yoghurt together, and serve over the warm pears.

MICROWAVE

1 Place the pears and honey in a microwave-safe container and cook on HIGH (100%) for 4 minutes.
2 Allow the pears to cool slightly. Mix the passionfruit and yoghurt together, and serve over the warm pears.

Variation

Nectarines or peaches can stand in for pears. The poaching time will vary depending on the ripeness of the fruit (the riper the fruit the higher the sugar content).

Hint

Fresh passionfruit can be frozen in its shell.

Quince with Raisins & Orange Sauce

The quince is a member of the rose family. When cooked, the flesh turns a soft pink, which adds an exotic touch to many sweet dishes.

Serves 2–4

¹/₂ cup raisins

2 tbsp water

4 small quinces, peeled and sliced very thinly

¹/₂ cup skim milk

50 g ricotta

¹/₃ cup plain low-fat yoghurt

juice of 1 orange

1–2 tsp orange zest

Energy:	1270 kJ/300 kCal
Fat:	4 g
Carbohydrate:	58 g
Fibre:	15 g

This dish is particularly rich in fibre and vitamin C, and also provides a good dose of calcium for healthy bones.

CONVENTIONAL

1 Heat the raisins with the water in a small saucepan over medium heat for 5–6 minutes until they are plump. Allow to cool.
2 Place the quinces and raisins in a bowl.
3 In a bowl mix together the milk, ricotta and yoghurt. Add the orange juice and zest. Use a stab mixer to ensure the mixture is smooth and well combined.
4 Add the quince and heat for 5–10 minutes with the raisins to increase the sweetness of the fruit, stirring regularly.
5 Spoon over the orange sauce.

MICROWAVE

1 Heat the raisins with the water in a microwave-safe container on HIGH (100%) for 1–2 minutes until the raisins are plump. Allow to cool.
2 Place the quinces with the raisins in a container and allow to stand covered.
3 In a bowl mix together the milk, ricotta and plain yoghurt. Add the orange juice and zest. Use a stab mixer to ensure the mixture is smooth and well combined.
4 Heat the quince with raisins on HIGH (100%) for 5 minutes to increase the sweetness of the fruit.
5 Spoon over the orange sauce.

Hint

Sliced, fragrant quinces are easily cooked in the microwave oven as they are too hard and sour to eat raw.

Poached Pears in Apple & Blackcurrant Juice

Energy: 830 kJ/200 kCal
Fat: 0.5 g
Carbohydrate: 38 g
Fibre: 3 g

Blackcurrant juice is one of nature's richest sources of vitamin C. One serve of this dish will more than meet your daily vitamin C needs.

Serves 2

1 cup blackcurrant juice

2 cloves

2 pears, peeled, cored and sliced

1 cup low-fat yoghurt

CONVENTIONAL

1 In a medium-sized saucepan, bring the blackcurrant juice and cloves to the boil. Add the pears and cover. Cook on medium heat for 35–40 minutes, stirring occasionally.
2 Remove from heat, and allow the pears to cool in the syrup. Remove the cloves.
3 Serve with yoghurt.

MICROWAVE

1 Place the blackcurrant juice, cloves and pears in a medium-sized microwave-safe container, and cook on HIGH (100%) for 5–7 minutes. Remove the cloves.
2 Remove from the microwave oven, and allow the pears to cool in the syrup.
3 Serve with yoghurt.

Variation

Garnish with fresh blackcurrants when they are in season.

Colourful Compote of Apple, Rhubarb & Pear

*A versatile preparation of fresh fruit that can be served hot or cold, with custard or **Ricotta Cream** (page 184). Serve for breakfast or as a dessert.*

Serves 2–4

2 cooking apples, peeled, cored and cut into chunky slices

1 large pear, peeled, cored and sliced

1½ cups apple juice (conventional method); 1 cup apple juice (microwave)

1 stick cinnamon or ½ tsp ground cinnamon

zest of 1 orange

½ bunch rhubarb, trimmed, washed and cut into 5 cm lengths

Energy:	690 kJ/165 kCal
Fat:	–
Carbohydrate:	40 g
Fibre:	6 g

Try this compote on your favourite cereal for breakfast, or use to top pancakes or muffins.

CONVENTIONAL

1 Place the apple and pear in a saucepan with the apple juice, cinnamon stick and zest and simmer for 10 minutes until the fruit is tender.
2 Add the rhubarb, cook for a further 5 minutes or until the fruit is just tender.
3 Stir through, cover and stand for 5 minutes before serving.

MICROWAVE

1 Place the apple and pear in a medium-sized microwave-safe container with the apple juice, cinnamon stick and zest.
2 Cover and cook on HIGH (100%) for 6–8 minutes until the fruit is just tender. Remove, scatter rhubarb around the sides. Cook for a further 3 minutes until the fruit is just tender.
3 Stir through and stand for 2 minutes before serving.

Hint

Always cover citrus fruits once the zest has been removed, as they dry out quickly.

Honeyed Brandied Pineapple

Many people are lazy about peeling fruit, but these days you can buy fruits like pineapple ready-peeled from your local supermarket. They are low in kilojoules and high in vitamins and flavour.

Energy: 375 kJ/90 kCal
Fat: –
Carbohydrate: 21 g
Fibre: 3 g

Pineapples are rich in vitamin C, particularly when fresh.

Variations

1 tbsp sultanas.

1 tbsp orange zest.

Hints

- The best time for pineapples is from mid-October to April. Select a pineapple for its aroma and ensure that the underneath stem is a creamy colour.
- Use your microwave during the hot weather to keep your kitchen cool.
- Make honey more manageable by heating on HIGH (100%) for 20–30 seconds in the microwave before using.

Serves 4–6

500 g pineapple, peeled and sliced

light spray oil

1 tbsp brandy or rum

1 tbsp honey

1 tsp cinnamon

Ricotta Cream (page 184) for serving

CONVENTIONAL

1 Preheat the oven to 250°C. Lightly spray an ovenproof dish with oil.
2 Cut the pineapples slices in half and place in the dish. Sprinkle with brandy. Drizzle with honey.
3 Dust with cinnamon, and bake for 20 minutes until brown and bubbling. Serve with **Ricotta Cream**.

MICROWAVE

1 Lightly oil a small ovenproof glass dish.
2 Cut the pineapple slices in half and place in the dish.
3 Sprinkle with brandy. Drizzle with honey.
4 Dust with cinnamon, and cover and cook on HIGH (100%) for 8 minutes. Allow to stand for 2 minutes, and serve with **Ricotta Cream**.

Tropical Salsa

Salsa simply means sauce, which can be either cooked or raw.
I like to use salsas to add a burst of fresh flavour to some dishes.

Serves 4–6

400 g peeled and diced pineapple

200 g peeled and diced pawpaw

150 g peeled and diced green mango

300 g peeled and diced watermelon

$1/2$ cup finely chopped mint

2 tbsp lime juice

CONVENTIONAL

1 Mix the prepared fruit in a large bowl.
2 Toss with mint and juice. Serve with cakes, custards
   and nuts.

Energy:	390 kJ/90 kCal
Fat:	–
Carbohydrate:	20 g
Fibre:	4 g

Variation

Use any seasonal tropical fruits available.

Hint

Look out for seedless watermelon.

Chilled Seasonal Fruit Bowl

The quantities for this treat will vary depending on the number of serves required. It's delicious on a hot afternoon.

Energy: 285 kJ/70 kCal
Fat: –
Carbohydrate: 15 g
Fibre: 4 g

Serves 4

½ pink or champagne watermelon

200 g grapes

3 passionfruit

2 oranges

CONVENTIONAL

1 Remove the pips from the watermelon and cut into bite-sized pieces. Place in a large bowl.
2 Remove the grapes from the stalks and add to the bowl. Add the passionfruit pulp. Segment the oranges and add to the bowl.
3 Toss the fruit and place in the freezer for 1–2 hours until icy.
4 Serve with vanilla-flavoured low-fat yoghurt.

Hint

Many fruits freeze well — frozen strawberries, bananas and mangoes can be added to this fruit bowl.

Pickled Peaches

Pickles are of Indian origin and may be made from fruit or vegetables or a mixture of both. They make good aperitifs, and can be served with cold meats, cheese and curries.

Serves 3–4

½ cup balsamic vinegar

1¾ cup brown sugar

½ tsp ground ginger

1 stick cinnamon

6 whole cloves

3 large peaches or nectarines, peeled and quartered

Energy:	275 kJ/65 kCal
Fat:	–
Carbohydrate:	15 g
Fibre:	1 g

Like most orange fruits and vegetables, peaches are a good source of the antioxidant vitamin A in the form of carotene.

CONVENTIONAL

1 Combine the vinegar, sugar, ginger, cinnamon stick and cloves in a large saucepan.
2 Heat to boiling. Reduce the heat, cover and simmer for 5 minutes.
3 Add the peaches, re-cover, and simmer for 10 minutes until the peaches are tender. Allow to stand for 30 minutes. Serve warm or chilled.

MICROWAVE

1 Combine the vinegar, sugar, ginger, cinnamon stick and cloves in a 2 litre microwave-safe jug. Cover with plastic wrap.
2 Cook on HIGH (100%) for 4 minutes to dissolve the sugar.
3 Add the peaches and stir through. Re-cover the jug and cook on HIGH (100%) for 5 minutes, stirring halfway through the cooking time. Allow to stand for 30 minutes. Serve warm or chilled.

Variation

Plums may be substituted for the peaches.

Hint

Store in sealed bottles in your refrigerator.

Tropical Delight

The convenience of canned fruit in natural juice is that you can enjoy your favourite fruits all year round.

Energy: 300 kJ/70 kCal
Fat: –
Carbohydrate: 15 g
Fibre: 2 g

All Australians should be eating at least three serves of fruit each day — this is a delicious way to add to that tally.

Serves 4

1 (420 g) can unsweetened tropical fruit, drained

zest and juice of 1 orange

2 egg whites

1 tbsp castor sugar

1 tsp cornflour

cinnamon (microwave method only)

CONVENTIONAL

1 Preheat the oven to 180°C.
2 Place the fruit and zest in an ovenproof dish.
3 Beat the egg whites in a clean mixing bowl until stiff peaks form. Gradually add the sugar and cornflour, and stir in the juice.
4 Spoon the meringue over the fruit and bake for 10 minutes or until lightly browned. Serve hot or cold.

MICROWAVE

1 Place the fruit and zest in a microwave-safe dish.
2 Beat the egg whites in a clean mixing bowl until stiff peaks form. Gradually add the sugar and cornflour, and stir in the juice.
3 Spoon the meringue over the fruit.
4 Put the dish off-centre, elevated, on a rack in a microwave oven. Cook on HIGH (100%) for 1–1^{1}/2 minutes until the meringue is just firm. Sprinkle over the cinnamon. Cool slightly, and serve while warm.

Variation

• Use any 425 g can of fruit in place of tropical fruit.
• Replace the ovenproof dish with 4 small (125–180 ml capacity) ramekins.

Hint

Dust the mirowave meringues with cinnamon to lightly brown.

Middle Eastern Dried Fruit Salad

Rosewater is an extract used for flavouring in the Middle East, the Balkans and India. It is available from Middle Eastern grocery stores and good delis.

Serves 4

1/2 tsp ground allspice

1/2 stick cinnamon

100 g dried figs

100 g dried apricots

100 g dates, pitted

2 wide strips orange zest

2 cups orange juice

1 tsp honey

1/2–1 tsp rosewater

yoghurt for serving

Energy:	930 kJ/220 kCal
Fat:	–
Carbohydrate:	53 g
Fibre:	9 g

Dried fruit is an excellent source of soluble fibre, iron and zinc, important minerals for maximising energy levels and preventing illness.

CONVENTIONAL

1 Place all the ingredients except the yoghurt in a medium-sized saucepan and slowly bring to a simmer.
2 Cook over low heat, for 15 minutes, stirring occasionally.
3 Take off the heat, and remove the cinnamon stick and zest. Serve warm or cold with a dollop of yoghurt.

MICROWAVE

1 Place all the ingredients except the yoghurt into a 1 litre microwave-safe jug.
2 Cover with plastic wrap, and cook on HIGH (100%) for 5 minutes.
3 Allow to stand for 5 minutes. Remove the cinnamon stick and zest. Serve warm or cold with a dollop of yoghurt.

Variation

Garnish with 1 tbsp whole blanched almonds.

Hints

- *To plump up dried fruit in the microwave, place in a jug, cover with water, black tea or fruit juice and cook on HIGH (100%) for 5 minutes.*
- *This salad improves in flavour if stored in the fridge for several weeks.*

Fruity Survival Snack

Pack this into lunches or hampers when you are travelling. You can vary the dried fruit and nuts to taste.

Energy: 815 kJ/195 kCal
Fat: 8 g
Carbohydrate: 27 g
Fibre: 4 g

Snacking on high-fibre, low-fat foods is essential for maintaining energy and blood glucose levels, and preventing overeating at the end of the day.

Serves 1–2

$1/4$ cup popping corn

1 tsp water

1 cup dried fruit medley

$1/2$ cup unsalted peanuts

MICROWAVE

1 Place the popcorn and water in an oven bag. Tie tightly with a rubber band.
2 Cook on HIGH (100%) for 3–4 minutes.
3 Combine the popcorn with the fruit medley and nuts.

Hint

Traditional cooking is not recommended due to the quantity of oil needed to cook popcorn.

BREAKFASTS & BRUNCHES

BREAKFASTS & BRUNCHES

Breakfast is not Australians' favourite meal of the day, with large percentages of adults and children skipping breakfast entirely, and less than 70 per cent eating breakfast every day. A high-carbohydrate meal to start the day helps ensure that your blood glucose levels are topped up for maximum energy levels and great concentration.

To achieve your maximum energy levels each day it is important to meet your carbohydrate needs. A breakfast of cereal, toast and fruit can contribute one-third of daily carbohydrate needs. For those of us whose activity is more brain oriented, nutrition research has found that people who eat a balanced breakfast can concentrate better and are more efficient at their work than those who skip breakfast. If you are expected to perform well in the office, or want your kids to think smart at school, we recommend that you have breakfast. If you skip breakfast to lose weight, think again. A low-fat high-carbohydrate, fibre-rich breakfast is more likely to help you keep body-fat levels under control than no breakfast. Eating breakfast helps boosts your metabolic rate, resulting in more effective energy usage each day. It can also prevent you overeating later in the day when your hunger gets out of control, and high-fat snacks such as chocolate, doughnuts, cakes and biscuits become very tempting. If you have embarked on a morning exercise programme to lose weight, then breakfast is vital for proper recovery and great energy levels for the rest of the day.

One of the most important things about the breakfast you choose is that you enjoy it! The second is that you should look for foods providing plenty of carbohydrate, a wide variety of vitamins and minerals, dietary fibre and very little fat. Try some of our great ideas for breakfast staples, quick brunches and snappy snacks.

Damper

Traditionally damper is cooked in a billy can for several hours, and served with sweet black tea in the outback. This is an easier version. It toasts well when stale.

Makes 12 slices

2 cups self-raising wholemeal flour

2 cups self-raising flour

1 tsp baking powder (microwave method only)

300 ml skim milk (conventional method); 1 cup skim milk (microwave)

$^1/_2$ cup natural low-fat yoghurt

extra milk

Energy: 675 kJ/162 kCal
Fat: 1 g
Carbohydrate: 31 g
Fibre: 4 g

CONVENTIONAL

1 Preheat the oven to 200°C.
2 In a mixing bowl sift together the flours and make a well in the centre. Stir in the milk and yoghurt to make a soft dough.
3 Turn onto a floured board and pat into a round shape. Do not knead.
4 Glaze with milk, and dust with spices or seeds if desired (see variation). Place onto a sheet of baking paper and then put on a baking tray. Mark 4–6 wedges with a knife.
5 Bake for 10 minutes, then reduce the temperature to 180°C and bake for a further 40–45 minutes, or until the top is golden brown and makes a hollow sound when tapped.

MICROWAVE

1 In a mixing bowl sift together the flours and baking powder.
2 In a separate mixing bowl combine the milk and yoghurt.
3 Make a well in the centre of the flour and stir in the milk mixture to make a soft dough.
4 Turn out onto a floured board and pat into a 5–6 cm round shape. (It spreads a lot as it cooks.) Do not knead.
5 Glaze with milk, dust with spice, and place onto a piece of paper towel or baking paper. Mark 4–6 wedges with a knife.
6 Place the damper in the microwave, elevated on a roasting rack, off centre of the turntable, and cook on HIGH (100%) for 5–6 minutes.
7 Move the damper to the other side of the turntable and microwave for a further 5–6 minutes on HIGH (100%).
8 Remove from the oven and allow to stand, covered with a tea towel, to cool.

Variations

- Add $3/4$ cup of dried fruit to the flours.
- Add $3/4$ cup sweet corn kernels and $1/4$ cup diced red capsicum to the flours before adding the liquid.
- Keep this low in fat by topping with tomato, basil and ricotta, or lean ham and mustard.

Hints

- *The dough can be dusted with paprika, poppyseed, sesame seeds or cinnamon (if making a fruit loaf).*
- *To make a sweeter-tasting plain or fruit loaf, use vanilla-flavoured yoghurt instead of plain.*

One-bowl Breakfast

Serves 1

Energy: 1124 kJ/270 kCal
Fat: 4 g
Carbohydrate: 48 g
Fibre: 6 g

A complete meal with lots of fibre, is rich in carbohydrates and low in fat. This breakfast also provides the important minerals, iron and calcium.

1 can (40 g) tropical fruit in natural juice

1 cup oat bran cereal or cereal of your choice (Weetbix, wheat flakes or rolled oats are good)

1/2 cup fruit yoghurt

1/2 tbsp chopped nuts

CONVENTIONAL

1 Combine all the ingredients except the nuts in a bowl.
2 Sprinkle with nuts to serve.

Variations

- Instead of canned fruit, use 1/2 cup dried mixed fruit.

- Add a piece of fresh fruit of your choice, for example, banana, apple, pear or stone fruit. Sprinkle 1–2 tsp of shredded coconut over the top.

Hint

*Low-fat natural yoghurt is a great substitute for cream. Combine with 1 tbsp honey and serve with grilled fruits, or **Poached Pears in Apple & Blackcurrant Juice** (page 118), or simply warm some strawberries and orange juice and drizzle over the top. Delicious!*

Apricot & Banana Kick Start

Bananas are rich in carbohydrates so they make an ideal between-meal snack to give you an energy boost. Here is a recipe for a simple start to the day — a drink packed with dietary fibre.

Serves 2, or 1 very hungry person

1 tsp vanilla essence

1 banana

2 tbsp smooth ricotta

1 tsp evaporated skim milk or skim milk

100 g canned apricots in juice

CONVENTIONAL

1   Place all the ingredients in a jug.
2   Blend until smooth with a stab mixer. Pour into a chilled glass to serve.

Energy: 1090 kJ/260 kCal
Fat: 5 g
Carbohydrate: 44 g
Fibre: 5 g

This high-fibre drink is a great source of calcium and phosphorous for strong bones. An excellent drink for kids who are fussy eaters.

Variation

You can also use a blender to mix the drink. Freeze in a glass for a summer snack.

Hint

Try fresh strawberries, raspberries, blueberries, canned peaches and plums in place of the banana.

Basic Pancake Mix

Pancakes are an excellent meal or snack before sport and a great after-school filler for the kids. They are rich in carbohydrates and low in fat, so keep the toppings healthy — go for jams, fruit spread, ricotta, banana, berries or even a dash of maple syrup.

Energy:	220 kJ/50 kCal
Fat:	0.5 g
Carbohydrate:	9 g
Fibre:	1 g

Variation

Mixed dried fruit may be added to the batter, or lemon, lime or orange zest.

Hint

Freeze unused pancakes in an airtight container. Place a piece of paper towel or greaseproof paper in between each to prevent sticking. This also allows one or two pancakes to be easily removed for a single serving. Reheat in the microwave for 30–40 seconds on HIGH (100%).

Makes 12

$3/4$ cup self-raising flour

$1/4$ cup self-raising wholemeal flour or $1/4$ cup rice flour

50 g smooth ricotta

$1^1/4$ cups skim milk

1 egg white

spray olive oil

CONVENTIONAL

1 In a mixing bowl sift both the flours together.
2 In a clean mixing bowl beat together the ricotta, skim milk and egg white.
3 Pour a little of the cheese mixture into the flour and stir carefully. Gradually add the rest of the cheese mixture to form a batter. Mix until the batter is smooth.
4 Spray a non-stick frypan with olive oil and heat. Pour $3/4$ cup batter to form a pancake about 10–15 cm in size. Cook until the batter bubbles, then flip the pancake over and cook the other side until golden brown.

Polenta

Polenta is a cornmeal porridge that is a basic dish of northern Italy. It is very versatile and can be served with a sweet or savoury sauce, or as a base for cheese and salad.

Makes 18 triangles

2$\frac{1}{2}$ cups water, beef or chicken stock

1 cup instant polenta

Chilli Ginger Jam (page 176) or **Tomato Jam** (page 175)

Energy:	515 kJ/120 kCal
Fat:	1 g
Carbohydrate:	26 g
Fibre:	1 g

CONVENTIONAL

1 Bring the water or stock to the boil in a saucepan.
2 Add the polenta slowly, whisking continually to ensure that no lumps form.
3 Simmer for 5 minutes, stirring constantly until the polenta leaves the side of the pan.
4 Lightly oil a 20 cm × 5 cm pan. Pour the polenta into the pan and smooth the top with a spatula. Refrigerate until set, 3–4 hours.
5 Cut into 9 squares, then into 18 triangles. Heat a chargrill or frypan and cook until the triangles are a golden brown colour. Serve with **Chilli Ginger Jam** or **Tomato Jam**.

MICROWAVE

1 Heat the water or stock in a 2 litre microwave-safe jug on HIGH (100%) for 5 minutes.
2 Add the polenta slowly, whisking continually until combined. Return to the microwave, cover and cook on HIGH (100%) for 2 minutes. Remove, stir again, cover and cook on MEDIUM HIGH (70–80%) for 3–4 minutes.
3 Spoon into a lightly oiled 23 cm glass pie dish and smooth the top with a spatula. Refrigerate until set, 3–4 hours.
4 Cut into 18 triangles. Cover lightly with plastic film. Put into a microwave oven on a roasting rack, and cook on HIGH (100%) for 5–6 minutes. Serve with **Chilli Ginger Jam** or **Tomato Jam**.

Variation

Milk may be used in place of water for desserts.

Pumpkin Loaf

The Queensland blue with its green–blue thick skin is the most popular pumpkin in Australia. It is sweet tasting and may be used in cakes, pies or scones or cooked as a vegetable.

Energy: 555 kJ/130 kCal
Fat: 3 g
Carbohydrate: 21 g
Fibre: 4 g

Another fibre-rich snack that is high in vitamin A in the form of carotenes from the pumpkin.

Variation

Use cooked sweet potato in place of the pumpkin.

Hint

Sprinkle poppyseeds over the top before baking. Pumpkin seeds maybe toasted in the oven for a delicious nutty flavour. Use in place of high-fat nuts for snacking. Place pumpkin seeds in a microwave-safe bowl and microwave on HIGH (100%) for 8–10 minutes.

Serves 12

300 g pumpkin, peeled, seeded and sliced

450 g (3 cups) self-raising wholemeal flour

1 tsp baking powder

1 tbsp oil

1/2 cup low-fat milk

1 egg

CONVENTIONAL

1 Preheat the oven to 200°C. Lightly grease a 15 cm long loaf tin with spray oil and line with baking paper.
2 Place the pumpkin in a some water and bring to the boil. Cook the pumpkin until soft, 10–15 minutes. Cool and mash.
3 Sift the flour and baking powder together in a mixing bowl.
4 In a separate mixing bowl combine the oil, milk, egg and cooled mashed pumpkin. Add the flour to the pumpkin mixture and stir in a cutting action with a flat-bladed knife until combined.
5 Bring the dough together with your hands and lightly knead. Place in the tin and spray with oil.
6 Bake for 20 minutes.

Orange Poppyseed Loaf

The main varieties of oranges grown in Australia are valencia (summer) and navel (winter). Also good for eating and including in cakes are blood oranges, which have flecks of red throughout their juicy flesh.

2 cups plain flour

1 cup wholemeal plain flour

1 tbsp baking powder

1 egg

1 tbsp castor sugar

$^1/_2$ cup vanilla low-fat yoghurt

zest and juice of 1 orange

1 cup low-fat milk

2 tbsp poppyseeds

Energy:	350 kJ/85 kCal
Fat:	2 g
Carbohydrate:	12 g
Fibre:	1 g

Poppyseeds are rich in calcium. However, given the small amounts that are generally consumed, and the fact that many pass through the gut undigested, they are not considered a useful source of dietary calcium.

CONVENTIONAL

1 Preheat the oven to 180°C. Lightly oil a 15 cm × 5 cm loaf tin.
2 In a mixing bowl sift together the two flours and baking powder.
3 In a separate mixing bowl beat the egg and sugar until light and creamy. Add the yoghurt, juice and zest.
4 Mix the flour and the milk into the orange mixture in alternate lots, then add the poppyseeds and mix thoroughly.
5 Pour into the tin, and bake for 60 minutes.

Variation

Use tangelos in place of oranges when they are in season.

Hint

When choosing oranges select those that feel heavy for their size — this ensures plenty of juice.

Munchy Honey Cakes

Ricotta, strictly speaking, is not cheese, as it is made from leftover whey from other cheese or milk. It may eaten fresh or cooked in sweet desserts and pasta dishes.

Energy: 670 kJ/160 kCal
Fat: 3 g
Carbohydrate: 25 g
Fibre: 0.5 g

Kids will love these nutritious versions of the 'Bananas in Pyjamas' favourite food. They are particularly rich in calcium and protein, ideal for growing bones.

Serves 2

$^1/_2$ cup smooth ricotta

$^1/_4$ cup low-fat skim milk

$^1/_3$ cup low-fat yoghurt

2 egg whites

$^1/_2$ cup rice flour

$^1/_2$ tsp baking powder

1 quantity **Banana, Prune & Coconut Topping** (page 142)

1 tbsp honey

CONVENTIONAL

1 In a bowl whisk together the ricotta, milk, and yoghurt.
2 In a separate clean bowl beat the egg whites until soft peaks form. Sift together the flour and baking powder in a separate bowl.
3 Fold the flour into the ricotta mixture, then carefully fold in the egg whites, until the mixture is evenly combined.
4 Heat a non-stick frypan and spray with a little oil.
5 Spoon 2 tbsp of batter into the pan and cook until golden brown on both sides.
6 Serve with the banana and prune mixture and honey.

Variation

Top with your favourite homemade jam (pages 171–8).

Ricotta & Strawberry Topping

Serves 1–2

2 tbsp natural low-fat yoghurt

1 tbsp honey

1 tsp vanilla essence

100 g smooth ricotta

3–4 strawberries, hulled and quartered

Energy:	510 kJ/120 kCal
Fat:	4 g
Carbohydrate:	14 g
Fibre:	–

A calcium and vitamin C rich, low-fat spread for toast, muffins, crumpets, pancakes and anything else you fancy.

CONVENTIONAL

1 Combine the yoghurt, honey, vanilla and ricotta. Add half of the strawberries, and carefully fold through.

2 Place the mixture on top of warm pancakes, crumpets or toast and top with the remaining strawberries.

Apple & Sultana Topping

Serves 1

$^1/_2$ apple, peeled, cored and cut into cubes

$^1/_4$ cup sultanas

$^1/_4$ tsp nutmeg or cinnamon

4 tbsp water

$^1/_2$ level tsp brown sugar

Energy: 305 kJ/75 kCal
Fat: –
Carbohydrate: 18 g
Fibre: 2 g

CONVENTIONAL

1 Place all the ingredients in a small saucepan. Cook the mixture over medium heat for 4–5 minutes until the apples have softened.
2 Pour over warm pancakes or crumpets.

MICROWAVE

1 Place all the ingredients in a microwave-safe bowl. Microwave on HIGH (100%) for 2 minutes until the apples have softened.
2 Pour over warm pancakes or crumpets.

Hint

Depending on the season and the sweetness of the variety of apple, you may need to increase or decrease the amount of sugar.

Hot Fruit & Nut Topping

The fruit is also delicious served cold.

Serves 2

¹/₄ cup diced apricots

¹/₄ cup sultanas

¹/₄ cup currants

1 tbsp each of pecans, almonds or hazelnuts

CONVENTIONAL

1 Place all the ingredients in a saucepan and gently warm the mixture through. This takes 3–4 minutes.
2 Pour over heated pancakes, crumpets or toast.

MICROWAVE

1 Place all the ingredients in a microwave-safe bowl and microwave on HIGH (100%) for 90 seconds.
2 Pour over heated pancakes, crumpets or toast.

Energy: 840 kJ/200 kCal
Fat: 5 g
Carbohydrate: 38 g
Fibre: 4 g

Dried fruit is a valuable source of soluble fibre and minerals such as iron.

Variation

Serve with ricotta.

Banana, Prune & Coconut Topping

Energy: 590 kJ/140 kCal
Fat: 2 g
Carbohydrate: 29 g
Fibre: 5 g

Rich in soluble fibre, this spread is delicious and great for keeping your gut healthy.

Serves 1–2

1 banana, mashed with a fork

$^1/_2$ cup prunes, pitted and roughly chopped

1 tsp vanilla essence

1 tbsp shredded coconut

CONVENTIONAL

1 Place all the ingredients in a saucepan and warm through over a medium heat for 2–3 minutes.
2 Serve on pancakes, crumpets or bread with a dollop of vanilla-flavoured yoghurt.

MICROWAVE

1 Combine the banana, prunes and vanilla and place on a pancake or crumpet. Cover with plastic wrap and elevate on a roasting rack in the microwave. Microwave on MEDIUM HIGH (70–80%) for 1 minute.
2 Serve with 1–2 tsp shredded coconut and a dollop of vanilla-flavoured yoghurt.

Hint

Freeze bananas for an iced summer treat.

Mandarine & Mint Topping

Use whatever citrus fruit is in season — try tangelos in winter and valencia oranges in summer.

Serves 1

1 mandarine, peeled and separated into segments

1 level tsp brown sugar

2–3 mint leaves

1 tsp water

2–3 mint leaves, extra

CONVENTIONAL

1 Place all the ingredients in a small saucepan and gently heat through for 2–4 minutes, stirring constantly. Remove from the heat once the mixture has come to the boil.

2 Remove the mint leaves and discard. Pour the mixture over heated pancakes or crumpets and garnish with fresh mint leaves and natural vanilla-flavoured yoghurt.

MICROWAVE

1 Place all the ingredients in a microwave-safe bowl and microwave on HIGH (100%) for 60 seconds.

2 Remove the mint leaves and discard. Pour the mixture over heated pancakes or crumpets and garnish with fresh mint leaves and natural vanilla-flavoured yoghurt.

Energy: 155 kJ/35 kCal
Fat: –
Carbohydrate: 8 g
Fibre: 1 g

This topping provides important vitamin C as well as fibre.

Hint

Oranges, mandarines and tangelos freeze successfully.

Sweet Banana Toppings

Australians consume a million bananas each week. While bananas are sweet they are almost fat free, making them useful for speedy sweet toppings. These suggestions are ideal for crackers, crisp bread or rice cakes.

Lightly mashed banana, cinnamon, and sultanas
Mashed banana and dates
Thinly spread Nutella and sliced bananas
Spread honey on rice cakes and top with sliced bananas

Other ideas
Low-fat cream cheese mixed with sugarless jam
Sliced strawberries in place of tomatoes
A thin spread of sweet apple or mango chutney
Thinly spread peanut butter combined with grated carrot

Hint

Freeze bananas for an iced summer treat.

PASTA & RICE

PASTA & RICE

While pasta and rice are well established as good and necessary carbohydrates in our daily diet as first courses and main meals, they are not generally considered dessert fare.

The pleasure of pasta is its versatility, with hundreds of different shapes to choose from, allowing you to experiment with more than just spaghetti.

Economical and filling, its nutritional value lies in its protein content, while its kilojoule count is low.

Egg noodles or pasta in a baked pudding make a colourful close to a light meal, and there are varied rice pudding ideas to draw upon.

Risotto, a favourite Italian first or main course, adapts beautifully to fruit, as you can see from the front cover!

Eat our desserts with 'gusto', and enjoy.

Pasta & Pecan Pudding

Noodle kugels are a Jewish dessert, and make a colourful finish to a light meal. They may be served hot or cold.

Serves 4–6

75 g macaroni

450 ml skim milk

1 Granny Smith apple, cored and chopped

50 g raisins, chopped

50 g pecans, chopped

1 tbsp brown sugar

1 tsp cinnamon

1 (55 g) egg, separated

1 Red Delicious apple, peeled and thinly sliced

Energy: 830 kJ/200 kCal
Fat: 7 g
Carbohydrate: 28 g
Fibre: 3 g

This pudding is a great way to add carbohydrates to a main meal, or to replenish energy stores after a hard exercise session.

CONVENTIONAL

1 Preheat the oven to 180°C. Lightly oil a cake ring.
2 Place the macaroni and milk in a saucepan and simmer gently for about 10 minutes.
3 Add the apple, raisins, pecans, sugar and cinnamon. Beat in the egg yolk.
4 In a clean mixing bowl beat the egg white until stiff peaks form. Fold into the mixture.
5 Pour into the cake ring and cook for 30 minutes. Place the sliced apple around the edge of the dish and bake for another 15 minutes.
6 Serve with vanilla-flavoured low-fat yoghurt.

MICROWAVE

1 Preheat the oven to 180°C. Lightly oil a cake ring.
2 Place the macaroni and milk into a 2 litre microwave and ovenproof safe container and simmer for 10 minutes on MEDIUM LOW (40%).
3 Add the apple, raisins, pecans, sugar and cinnamon. Beat in the egg yolk.
4 In a clean mixing bowl beat the egg whites until stiff peaks form. Fold into the mixture.
5 Pour into the cake ring and cook for 30 minutes. Place the sliced apple around the edge of the dish and bake for another 15 minutes.
6 Serve with vanilla-flavoured low-fat yoghurt.

Noodles Dolce Vita

A favourite noodle dish of New Yorkers.

Serves 2

150 g noodles or pasta bows

8 cups boiling water

1 tbsp margarine

2 tbsp sugar

$1/2$ tsp cinnamon

vanilla-flavoured low-fat yoghurt or ricotta

Energy: 960 kJ/230 kCal
Fat: 4 g
Carbohydrate: 40 g
Fibre: 2 g

Another great high-carbohydrate, low-fat dish for athletes, sports-people and growing kids, or pasta lovers.

CONVENTIONAL

1 Boil the pasta or noodles until tender in the boiling water. Drain and rinse. Divide between 2 large bowls.

2 In a small saucepan, melt the margarine, sprinkle in the sugar and cinnamon, stirring to blend well.

3 Drizzle over the top of the noodles, and top with yoghurt or **Ricotta Cream** (page 184).

Variation

Add nuts and fruit.

Summer Berry Risotto

If you lose your appetite when the 'heat is on', this dish is a good source of carbohydrates for energy.

Serves 8–10

1 cup Arborio rice

2 cups fruit juice or water

200 g vanilla-flavoured low-fat yoghurt

1 tsp lemon zest

1 punnet blueberries, rinsed

1 punnet raspberries, rinsed

1 punnet strawberries, rinsed and hulled

$1/2$ cup water

mint

extra strips of lemon zest

Energy: 475 kJ/115 kCal
Fat: –
Carbohydrate: 24 g
Fibre: 3 g

Most Australians don't eat enough carbohydrate. Combining fruit and rice makes for a tasty way of meeting carbohydrate needs with a minimum of fat and plenty of fibre.

CONVENTIONAL

1 Place the rice and juice in a medium-sized saucepan. Bring the water to the boil and then simmer, stirring occasionally, until the water is absorbed. Cool.

2 Stir through the yoghurt and lemon zest. Fold half of the berries through the rice carefully, so that you do not damage the fruit.

3 In a saucepan over medium heat, place the rest of the berries in the water and heat until the juice is just released. Puree and cool.

4 To serve, place a portion of risotto on a plate and pour the berry puree on the side. Garnish with mint and strips of lemon zest.

MICROWAVE

1   Place the rice and juice in a large microwave-safe bowl and cook on HIGH (100%) for 10 minutes. Stir with a fork, and cook for a further 2–3 minutes. Allow to stand and cool.
2   Stir through the yoghurt and lemon zest. Fold through half of the berries carefully. Try not to damage the fruit.
3   In a small microwave-safe container place the other half of the berries. Cook for 1–2 minutes on HIGH (100%) until juice is just released. Puree and cool.
4   To serve, place a portion of risotto on a plate and pour the berry puree on the side. Garnish with mint and strips of lemon zest.

Variation

Short-grain calrose rice grown in Australia makes a good risotto.

Hint

Use canned fruit when berries are out of season.

Persian Couscous

Couscous is actually classified as a pasta, and makes for a nice variation. It requires very little preparation.

Serves 4

1¹/₂ cups couscous

1¹/₂ cups boiling water (conventional method);
    1¹/₂ cups water (microwave)

spray oil (conventional method)

¹/₂ cup sultanas

¹/₂ cup diced dried peaches

¹/₂ cup diced dried figs

30 g flaked almonds

Energy: 1070 kJ/255 kCal
Fat: 3 g
Carbohydrate: 50 g
Fibre: 5 g

This dish provides iron and loads of carbohydrate but very little fat.

CONVENTIONAL

1 Place the couscous in a bowl, pour over the water and toss with a fork until it absorbs almost all of the liquid.
2 Heat some spray oil in a frypan and add the couscous. Stir constantly over low heat for 4 minutes.
3 Stir in the fruits and almonds and cook for a further 4–5 minutes until heated through, stirring regularly. Serve as a sweet or savoury dish.

MICROWAVE

1 Boil the water in the microwave and add the couscous. Fork through until the liquid is absorbed.
2 Cook on HIGH (100%) in the microwave for 60 seconds.
3 Stir in the fruits and almonds. Cover and cook on HIGH (100%) for 2 minutes. Serve as a sweet or savoury dish.

Variation

Pine nuts mix well with couscous.

Hint

Couscous reheats well in the microwave with the addition of 1 tbsp liquid. Reheat on MEDIUM (50–60%).

CHRISTMAS

TREATS

CHRISTMAS TREATS

Despite the Australian summer heat, 'old-fashioned' Christmas fare still appears annually. Christmas time is often a time of over-indulgence, when high-fat, high sugar and low-nutrition foods abound. If Christmas only consisted of Christmas Day this wouldn't be a problem; however, for many the festive season begins in November and ends in late January. This Christmas try some of our specially adapted recipes, stay active, and enjoy festive food without fear!

For those who like to participate in a 'Christmas in July' celebration, remember that dried fruits are higher in sugars than fresh, which increases their kilojoule count, so moderation is the key!

Christmas Cassata

Great for the hot Aussie Christmas climate.

Energy: 1025 kJ/245 kCal
Fat: 4 g
Carbohydrate: 28 g
Fibre: 1 g

A low-fat alternative to Christmas pudding for a hot Australian Christmas.

Serves 12

Sauce

2 tbsp chocolate drops

1 tbsp skim milk

Cassata

200 g fruit medley

2 tbsp raisins

2 tbsp brandy or essence

1 litre low-fat icecream

MICROWAVE

1 To make the sauce, place the chocolate drops and milk in a microwave-safe container. Place in the microwave and melt on MEDIUM (50%) for 45 seconds to 1 minute. Stir well to achieve a smooth liquid. (Or place the chocolate and milk in a double saucepan and melt over a low heat for 10–15 minutes.)

2 To make the cassata, mix the fruit medley, raisins and brandy together in a medium-sized microwave-safe bowl and cook on DEFROST (30%) for 6 minutes. Set aside to cool.

3 Soften the icecream by cooking on DEFROST (30%) for 1 minute. Line a 1.5 litre pudding basin with plastic wrap.

4 Fold the cooled fruit through the icecream, then spoon into the pudding basin and freeze overnight.

5 To serve, turn out the pudding onto a plate and pour the sauce over the top. Allow it to drizzle around the pudding. Decorate with Christmas tinsel stars.

Hint

A plastic-lined pudding basin makes it easier to pull out the frozen pudding from the bowl.

Festive Boiled Christmas Fruit Cake

Even in the most intense heat, Christmas traditions still take place. If it's hot, you may prefer to serve this old-fashioned cake in small individual portions.

Serves 8

2 cups dried fruit

¹/₄ cup dried apricots

2 cups soft breadcrumbs (stale rye bread will give the cake a dark colour)

1 cup skim milk with 1 tsp bicarbonate of soda dissolved in it

2 ripe bananas, mashed (almost black is ideal)

2 tsp mixed spice

2 tsp brandy or essence

Energy:	600 kJ/145 kCal
Fat:	0.5 g
Carbohydrate:	33 g
Fibre:	3 g

CONVENTIONAL

1 Preheat the oven to 150°C. Line and grease a 1 litre pudding basin or 8 custard cups (180 ml capacity).
2 Combine all the ingredients in a large mixing bowl.
3 Pour into a pudding basin or individual ramekins and cover the top with baking paper and foil.
4 Place in a pot of boiling water — the water should come halfway up the sides. Cover the dish and pot with foil and steam for 2 hours.
5 Invert onto a serving platter. Serve with **Custard** (page 182) or **Festive Fruit & Nut Sauce** (page 188).

MICROWAVE

1 Combine all the ingredients in a large mixing bowl.
2 Place in a large microwave-safe jug and cover with plastic wrap.
3 Microwave in the pudding bowl on DEFROST (30%) for 30 minutes. Allow to stand for 7 minutes.
4 Invert onto a serving platter. Serve with **Custard** (page 182) or **Festive Fruit & Nut Sauce** (page 188).

Last-minute Moist Christmas Cake

This cake is quick and easy to make if you run out of time before Christmas.

Serves 12

375 g mixed dried fruit

440 g can crushed pineapple in natural juice

$1/4$ cup squeezed orange juice

2 tsp mixed spice

1 cup dark jam

250 g pitted prunes, chopped

1 tsp bicarbonate of soda

2 cups self-raising wholemeal flour

2 egg whites

Low-Joule Jam (pages 170–8)

CONVENTIONAL

1 Place the dried fruit, pineapple and juice, orange juice, mixed spice, jam and prunes in a saucepan and cook over moderate heat. Bring to the boil, then reduce the heat and simmer uncovered for 5 minutes.

2 Remove from the heat, and transfer the mixture to a mixing bowl and allow to cool.

3 Preheat the oven to 180°C. Grease and line a square 18 cm cake tin.

4 Sift the bicarbonate of soda and flour together. In a clean bowl beat the egg whites until stiff peaks form.

5 Fold the egg whites into the fruit mixture and then the sifted flour. The mixture will be quite firm.

6 Spread into the tin and bake for $1^1/2$ hours.

7 Allow to cool thoroughly before inverting onto a platter. Lightly glaze with strained jam.

Energy: 980 kJ/235 kCal
Fat: 1 g
Carbohydrate: 53 g
Fibre: 6.5 g

Dried fruit like apricots and prunes provide iron, a mineral important in the transport of oxygen around the body.

MICROWAVE

1 Place the dried fruit, pineapple and juice, orange juice, mixed spice, jam and prunes in a large microwave-safe container. Cook uncovered on DEFROST (30%) for 7 minutes.

2 Remove from the heat, and transfer into a mixing bowl and allow to cool.

3 Sift the bicarbonate of soda and flour together. In a clean bowl beat the egg whites until stiff peaks form.

4 Fold the egg whites into the fruit mixture and then the sifted flour. The mixture will be quite firm.

5 Spread into a large microwave container lined with absorbent paper towels. Cover the top loosely with paper towel. Elevate the container off the centre of the turntable and cook on MEDIUM HIGH (70–80%) for 20 minutes, moving the container to the opposite side of the turntable halfway through the cooking time.

6 Allow to cool thoroughly before inverting onto a platter. Lightly glaze with strained jam.

True Blue Plum Pudding

Serves 10–12

1¹/₂ cups mixed dried fruit

200 g canned dark plums

1 cup reserved plum juice

1 tsp grated ginger

2 (55 g) eggs, lightly beaten

1¹/₂ cups self-raising flour, sifted

¹/₂ cup plain flour, sifted

1 tsp bicarbonate of soda, sifted

1 tbsp Parisian essence, more if desired

Energy: 715 kJ/170 kCal
Fat: 1 g
Carbohydrate: 37 g
Fibre: 2 g

Little Jack Horner would pull out plenty of carbohydrate, fibre, vitamins and minerals as well as the plum from this great pudding!

CONVENTIONAL

1 Preheat the oven to 180°C. Lightly grease a 3 litre pudding basin.
2 Place the dried fruit, plums, plum juice and ginger in a medium-sized saucepan and bring to the boil. Reduce the heat and simmer for 8–10 minutes. Transfer the fruit and syrup to a large mixing bowl and cool (the mixture can be cooled overnight).
3 Add the eggs to the cooled fruit mixture. Stir in the flours and bicarbonate of soda. Add the essence.
4 Spoon into the prepared pudding basin. Cover the top with foil and place in a deep-sided baking dish. Pour boiling water into the baking dish to reach halfway up the sides of the pudding basin.
5 Cook for 1 hour until cooked through. Serve with brandy custard.

MICROWAVE

1 Lightly grease and line a large microwave-safe glass jug with paper towels.
2 Place the dried fruits, plums, plum juice and ginger into a 2 litre microwave-safe bowl. Microwave for 2 minutes on HIGH (100%). Allow the mixture to cool (it can be cooled overnight).
3 Add the eggs to the cooled mixture. Stir in the flours and bicarbonate of soda. Add the essence. Pour into the jug and cover with plastic wrap.
4 Microwave on DEFROST (30%) for 10–15 minutes and allow to stand for 5 minutes. Serve with brandy custard.

Hint

Plum pudding made this way minimises the washing up.

Chocolate Christmas Stars

A sweet treat that is low in fat if you don't eat too many! Give them away to friends for the Christmas tree or table.

Makes 40 stars

$^1/_2$ cup castor sugar

75 g margarine

1 (55 g) egg

1 cup self-raising flour, sifted

1 tbsp self-raising wholemeal flour, sifted

50 g cocoa powder, sifted

3–4 red and green boiled lollies, crushed (for colour)

Per star

Energy:	170 kJ/40 kCal
Fat:	2 g
Carbohydrate:	5 g
Fibre:	–

CONVENTIONAL

1 Preheat the oven to 150°C. Line a baking tray with baking paper.

2 In a mixing bowl beat the sugar and margarine until light and creamy. Add the egg and mix well.

3 Sift in both the flours and cocoa. Beat until the mixture comes cleanly away from the side of the mixer. Add some water if the mixture is too dry.

4 Lightly flour the work bench and roll out the mixture to a thickness of 1 cm. Cut into star shapes with a 6 cm cutter. Carefully place on the tray.

5 Using a teaspoon, cut out a 1 cm sized round hole in the middle of the biscuit. Bake for 6–8 minutes.

6 Remove the biscuits from the oven and fill the centre with the crushed lollies (approximately $^1/_2$ tsp will be enough for each). Turn the oven up to 180°C and bake for a further 6–8 minutes, until the lollies have melted and biscuits are cooked.

Variation

30 g diet berry jam
Make a slight indentation on the top of the biscuit. Bake for 6–8 minutes at 150°C. Spoon $^1/_2$ tsp diet jam on the indentation. Return the biscuits to the oven and bake at 180°C for a further 6–8 minutes.

Hint

The biscuit mixture freezes well.

Festive Fruit Slice

If you don't want too rich a cake over the festive season this slice will fit the bill.

Serves 8

1¹/₂ cups wholemeal self-raising flour

200 g mixed fruit

1 (55 g) egg

1 tsp coconut essence

¹/₄ cup water

1 tbsp oil

2 tbsp honey

¹/₂ cup desiccated coconut, toasted

Energy: 380 kJ/90 kCal
Fat: 3 g
Carbohydrate: 15 g
Fibre: 2 g

CONVENTIONAL

1 Preheat the oven to 180°C. Lightly oil a 20 cm × 12 cm baking dish.
2 Combine the flour and fruit in a large mixing bowl.
3 In a separate bowl lightly beat the egg. Add the essence, water and oil. Mix into the dry ingredients.
4 Heat the honey over low heat until very thin and runny. Add to the mixture and stir until combined. Transfer the mixture to the baking dish.
5 Bake for 25 minutes or until the top is golden brown. Sprinkle with coconut.

Christmas Wreath

A healthy alternative over Christmas.

Serves 12

3 (55 g) eggs

1/2 cup self-raising flour

1/2 cup oatbran

1/2 tsp baking powder

1 tsp rum essence (optional)

75 g pecans

90 g sultanas

150 g raisins

150 g dates

50 g prunes

50 g apricots

Decoration

2 tbsp **Low-joule Jam** (pages 171–8)

50 g pecans

100 g glacé pineapple

50 g red glacé cherries

Energy: 875 kJ/210 kCal
Fat: 6 g
Carbohydrate: 35 g
Fibre: 4 g

All the dried fruit in this wreath makes it relatively high in iron, particularly if you have a glass of juice or fresh fruit with it to help the iron absorption.

CONVENTIONAL

1 Beat the eggs in a large mixing bowl. Lightly grease a 20 cm ring cake tin.
2 Fold in the flour, oatbran, baking powder and essence.
3 Mix in all the fruits and spoon the mixture into the tin. Bake for 45 minutes, then cool on a cake rack.
4 Invert on a serving plate when cold, and glaze with the strained jam. Decorate with the pecans and glacé fruits.

MICROWAVE

1 Beat the eggs in a large mixing bowl.
2 Fold in the flour, oatbran, baking powder and essence.
3 Mix in all the fruits and spoon into a microwave-safe cake container that has been lightly greased. Cook on MEDIUM (50–60%) for 10–12 minutes, then cool on a cake rack.
4 Invert on a serving plate when cold, and glaze with the jam. Decorate with the pecans and glacé fruits.

Hint

Add Parisian essence for a darker-coloured cake.

Fruity Bon Bons

A contemporary presentation of traditional mince pies.

Energy: 530 kJ/130 kCal
Fat: 4 g
Carbohydrate: 21 g
Fibre: 1.5 g

Fruit mince is a good source of carbohydrate and fibre and is low in fat.

Variation

1 Place the filo pastry in a well-greased muffin pan.
2 Spoon 1 tbsp of the fruit mince and almond mixture into the pastry shells.
3 Bake in a preheated 180°C oven until golden brown.

Serves 10

10 sheets filo pastry
1 (250 g) jar fruit mince
2 tbsp almond slivers

CONVENTIONAL

1 Preheat the oven to 190°C.
2 Fold the filo sheets in half, and then in half again. The pastry parcel will be approximately 5 cm wide.
3 Place 1 tbsp of the fruit mince onto one side of the pastry, add a few almond slivers, and roll up. Tie the ends with raffia or string. Transfer the rolls onto a lined baking tray. Repeat with the remaining pastry.
4 Bake for 15 minutes until lightly golden.

Meringue Stars

Meringues are a delicious way to serve fresh fruit and are virtually fat free! People with diabetes may need to limit their intake of these.

Makes 12 small stars

5 egg whites

2 tbsp castor sugar

3 tsp custard powder

1¹/₂ tsp lemon juice

250 g berries of your choice (raspberries, blackberries and blueberries)

Energy:	75 kJ/18 kCal
Fat:	–
Carbohydrate:	3 g
Fibre:	–

CONVENTIONAL

1 Preheat the oven to 150°C. Line a baking tray with baking paper.
2 Whisk the egg whites at high speed until soft peaks form. Slowly add the sugar and beat until the mixture is thick and glossy.
3 Beat in the custard powder and lemon juice.
4 Fill a piping bag fitted with your choice of nozzle with the meringue. Pipe the meringue into individual star shapes, about 5–7 cm in diameter. Leave a small hole in the centre for the fruit.
5 Bake for 10–12 minutes. Allow to cool.
6 Heat the berries in a small saucepan over a low heat for 5 minutes until they soften to form a sauce.
7 Pour around the cooled stars.

CHUTNEYS & JAMS

CHUTNEYS & JAMS

Chutneys, jams, pickles and other condiments make excellent flavour enhancers for low-fat dishes, and can be used in place of butter or margarine for moist sandwiches. They are an ideal way to make use of summer's bounty, when fruit and vegetables are plentiful and cheap. We have included recipes for old favourites such as apple chutney, marmalade and orange pickle.

Select ripe undamaged fruit to give maximum sweetness and enhance it with 50 ml of your favourite liqueur.

The key to making jam is pectin. Pectin is a substance found in the seeds, skins and cores of fruit that dissolves in the presence of sugar, acid and heat, and, on cooling, forms a gel. Use just ripe or slightly under-ripe fruit for the most pectin. If the fruit is low in pectin or acid, you need to add lemon juice or combine it with another fruit that is high in pectin.

Citrus fruit, apples, blackcurrants, plums, crabapples and quinces all have a high pectin content. Fruits low in pectin include strawberries, cherries, peaches, rhubarb (not strictly a fruit) and pears. For best results, make jam in small batches. We add pectin to take the guesswork out of the setting properties of the preserve or jam.

This is a food area where the microwave really comes into its own. You will find that the shortened cooking times enhance the flavour, colour and shape of the fruit. Cleaning up is easy because there is no scorching, sticking or boiling over.

To make small quantities (1 kg at a time) in a microwave, use a large 2 litre ovenproof glass jug or bowl so the mixture won't boil over. If this looks likely, open the door and stir to distribute the heat evenly.

The combined jam ingredients should only be about 5 cm deep in the saucepan.

You'll need a thermometer, baking tray for sterilising bottles, a heat-resistant dish, a large, wide, heavy-based saucepan (to distribute heat evenly — the wide surface area of the saucepan allows for fast evaporation and quick cooling), a wooden spoon, a ladle and jars for bottling.

Apple Chutney

This is an old-fashioned chutney that goes well with meat, cheese and curry.

Makes 2³/₄ cups

500 g Granny Smith apples, peeled, cored and chopped
¹/₄ cup dark brown sugar
1 medium-sized onion, finely chopped
1 cup raisins
¹/₂ cup diced red or green capsicum
¹/₂ cup balsamic or white wine vinegar
¹/₂ tsp each of ginger, allspice and mustard seeds
¹/₄ tsp chilli flakes

Each 25 g serve
Energy: 90 kJ/20 kCal
Fat: —
Carbohydrate: 5 g
Fibre: 0.5 g

CONVENTIONAL

1 Place the apples, sugar, onion, raisins, capsicum, vinegar, ginger, allspice, mustard seeds and chilli flakes in a medium-sized saucepan. Bring to the boil, stirring frequently.
2 Reduce the heat and simmer uncovered for 50 minutes or until the mixture is thickened. Stir regularly to prevent sticking. Allow to stand for 10 minutes.
3 Cool, and store in the refrigerator in sterilised jars.

MICROWAVE

1 Place the apples, sugar, onion, raisins, capsicum, vinegar, ginger, allspice, mustard seeds and chilli flakes in a 2 litre microwave-safe jug. Stir until well mixed.
2 Cover with plastic wrap. Cook on HIGH (100%) for 10 minutes.
3 Stir well, re-cover, and cook on MEDIUM HIGH (70–80%) for a further 10 minutes.
4 Allow to stand for 10 minutes. Cool, and store in the refrigerator in sterilised jars.

Hints

- To sterilise bottles, half-fill the bottle with water and bring to the boil in a large pot filled with water. Drain the water, and invert the bottle on clean paper towels to dry.
- To prevent raisins from sticking to a knife, toss with 1 tsp vegetable oil.

Three-fruit Marmalade

Makes 2 cups

1 (200 g) orange, cut into 0.5 cm dice, skin on

1 (170 g) lemon, cut into 0.5 cm dice, skin on

1 (140 g) grapefruit, cut into 0.5 cm dice, without the pith/skin

1½ cups water

2 heaped tbsp low-joule jelly crystals (orange, lemon or lime)

MICROWAVE

1 Place the fruit and water in a 2 litre microwave-safe glass jug.
2 Cover and cook on HIGH (100%) for 13 minutes.
3 Stir in the jelly crystals and cook, uncovered, for 12 minutes, stirring occasionally. Cool, and bottle in sterilised jars.

Each 25 g serve

Energy:	30 kJ/6 kCal
Fat:	– g
Carbohydrate:	1 g
Fibre:	0.5 g

Oranges, lemons and grapefruit are rich in pectin, a type of soluble dietary fibre. Soluble fibre is believed to help lower blood cholesterol levels. Fruit is also rich in many types of antioxidants, which can help reduce the risk of heart disease.

Trio of Summer Berries Jam

This jam is a berried treasure for summer holidays.

Each 25 g serve

Energy: 65 kJ/15 kCal
Fat: –
Carbohydrate: 3 g
Fibre: 1 g

Keep this fibre-rich spread for winter as it is packed with vitamin C.

Makes 2 cups

250 g strawberries, rinsed and hulled

250 g raspberries, rinsed

250 g blackberries or blueberries, rinsed

$1/3$ cup fresh orange juice

$1/3$ cup castor sugar

2 heaped tbsp pectin

CONVENTIONAL

1 Combine the berries in a large saucepan and cook over a low heat for 6–8 minutes until the fruits soften.
2 Stir in the orange juice and sugar. Bring to the boil, then simmer for 20 minutes.
3 Stir in the pectin and simmer for a further 5 minutes.
4 Cool, and bottle in sterilised jars.

MICROWAVE

1 Place the berries and orange juice in a large microwave-safe container. Cover and cook on HIGH (100%) for 5 minutes.
2 Uncover, and stir through the sugar. Re-cover and cook for a further 5 minutes on HIGH (100%).
3 Uncover and stir through the pectin. Leave uncovered and cook for a further 5 minutes on HIGH (100%).
4 Cool, and bottle in sterilised jars.

Hint

Mix and match the berries of your choice. Frozen berries can be used in place of the fresh.

Glut Buster

An easy recipe for any summer fruit when it is abundant, ripe and cheap.

Makes 500 ml

500 g plums, peaches or nectarines, pitted and chopped

1 sweet orange, seeded and finely chopped

zest of 1 lemon

1 tbsp pectin

Each 25 g serve

Energy:	35 kJ/8 kCal
Fat:	–
Carbohydrate:	1.5 g
Fibre:	0.5 g

A fibre-rich, low-sugar spread or topping with no fat.

CONVENTIONAL

1 Place the plums, orange and zest in a medium-sized saucepan.
2 Bring to the boil, stirring constantly. Reduce the heat and simmer gently for 15–20 minutes, stirring regularly to prevent sticking.
3 Stir in the pectin and simmer for 5 minutes.
4 Cool, and bottle in sterilised jars.

MICROWAVE

1 Place the plums, orange and zest in a 2 litre microwave-safe glass jug.
2 Cover and cook on HIGH (100%) for 5 minutes.
3 Uncover, stir and cook on HIGH (100%) for 5 minutes.
4 Stir in the pectin and cook on HIGH (100%) for a further 5 minutes.
5 Cool, and bottle in sterilised jars.

Hint

There are over 200 varieties of stone fruit grown in Australia. They are suited to different climates, and ready for picking at different times, so you can enjoy stone fruit for a longer season.

Kiwifruit & Pineapple Jam

This jam is rather tart and doubles up as a salsa for pork, meats and poultry.

Makes 600 ml

500 g fresh pineapple, peeled and roughly chopped

500 g kiwifruit, peeled and chopped

25 g pectin

1 tbsp honey

CONVENTIONAL

1 Place all the ingredients in a heavy-based saucepan and bring to the boil.
2 Simmer for 15 minutes, stirring often, until the pineapple is tender. Cool, and bottle in sterilised jars.

MICROWAVE

1 Place the pineapple and kiwifruit in a 2 litre microwave-safe glass jug.
2 Cover with plastic wrap and cook on HIGH (100%) for 5 minutes.
3 Stir through and cook uncovered for 5 minutes.
4 Stir in the pectin and cook uncovered for 5 minutes.
5 Stir in the honey. Cool, and bottle in sterilised jars.

Hint

Kiwifruit makes a great snack. Remove the top from the fruit and scoop out the flesh with a spoon.

Tomato Jam

A sweet and spicy jam that's great with muffins, dampers and scones.

Makes 300 ml

500 g ripe Roma tomatoes

1 tbsp brown sugar

$^1/_2$ tsp mustard seeds

1 tbsp olive oil

1 tbsp balsamic vinegar

freshly ground pepper

Each 25 g serve

Energy:	55 kJ/15 kCal
Fat:	1 g
Carbohydrate:	1 g
Fibre:	0.5 g

Tomatoes are rich in lycopenes, which are believed to have strong antioxidant effects and may assist with the prevention of many cancers and heart disease.

CONVENTIONAL

1 Cut the tomatoes in half. Squeeze out and discard the seeds, and roughly chop the flesh.

2 Place the tomatoes in a medium-sized saucepan with the sugar, mustard seeds, oil and vinegar. Bring to the boil.

3 Lower the heat and simmer for 25 minutes, stirring often until thick. Season with pepper.

4 Cool, and store in a sterilised jar in the refrigerator.

MICROWAVE

1 Cut the tomatoes in half. Squeeze out and discard the seeds, and roughly chop the flesh.

2 Place the tomatoes in a medium-sized ovenproof glass jug with the sugar, mustard seeds, oil and vinegar.

3 Cook on HIGH (100%) for 15 minutes, stirring twice. Season with pepper.

4 Cool, and store in a sterilised jar in the refrigerator.

Hint

If you are peeling a large quantity of tomatoes, place them in a 180°C oven for 15 minutes or until the skins burst and slip off easily.

Chilli Ginger Jam

Try this jam with sausages, barbecued meats or roast lamb. For offal lovers, it is terrific with cold tongue.

Makes 2–2$^1/_2$ cups

1 kg Roma tomatoes

spray oil

1 tbsp olive oil

3 large cloves garlic, crushed

10 g piece ginger, finely chopped

$^1/_2$–1 tsp dried chilli flakes or to taste

2 tbsp balsamic vinegar

1 tbsp each of cumin, coriander and mustard seeds

CONVENTIONAL

1 Preheat the oven to 180°C.
2 Spray the tomatoes lightly with oil and roast for 20 minutes.
3 Remove the skins and discard. Set aside the flesh.
4 In a small blender combine the oil, garlic, ginger, chilli, vinegar, spices and mustard seeds. Blend until finely chopped.
5 Transfer the mixture to a medium-sized heavy-based saucepan. Add the tomatoes. Simmer over a low heat for 30–35 minutes until the liquid reduces to a thick, pulpy consistency. Stir several times during cooking to prevent sticking to the pan base.
6 Cool, and pour into sterilised bottles, and seal well. Store in the refrigerator for 1 month.

MICROWAVE

1 Cut the tomatoes in half and put on a foil-lined griller tray. Cook under moderate heat for 10–15 minutes or until the skins shrivel and blacken slightly.

2 Remove the skins and discard. Chop the flesh and set aside.

3 In a small blender combine the oil, garlic, ginger, chilli, vinegar, spices and mustard seeds. Blend until finely chopped.

4 Put the tomatoes and spice mixture into an 8 cup microwave-safe jug, and stir to combine. Cover the top with absorbent paper, place the jug in a microwave oven, and cook on HIGH (100%) for 10 minutes. Remove, stir, and cook for a further 5–7 minutes, until the mixture is thick and pulpy.

5 Cool, and pour into sterilised bottles, and seal well. Store in the refrigerator for 1 month.

Hint

Fresh ginger keeps very well in a screwtop jar in the fridge. Peel, then cover with dry sherry. The liquid also adds a spicy tang to stir-fries.

Orange Pickle Jam

A deliciously sweet spread on hot toast. Sealed in sterilised jars, this pickle will keep for 3 months in a cool spot. Great with a vegetarian curry or dhal and rice.

Makes 2 cups

6 thin-skinned valencia oranges

2 tbsp brown sugar

2 tbsp honey

$1/2$ cup balsamic vinegar

$1/2$ cup water

1 tbsp garam masala

CONVENTIONAL

1 Place the whole oranges in a large saucepan with enough warm water to cover. Cover the saucepan and simmer for 40 minutes. Drain, and leave until cool enough to handle.
2 In a medium-sized saucepan combine the sugar, honey, vinegar, water and garam masala and bring to the boil.
3 Cut the oranges into quarters and then into 2 cm pieces.
4 Return the oranges to the large saucepan. Pour the syrup mixture over, bring to a simmer over medium heat and cook uncovered for 30–35 minutes, stirring regularly. The orange rind should be tender.
5 Cool, then spoon the mixture into sterilised jars.

CONVENTIONAL/MICROWAVE

1 Place whole oranges in a large saucepan with enough warm water to cover. Cover and simmer for 40 minutes.
2 Drain and leave until cool enough to handle.
3 Place the sugar, honey, vinegar, water and spices in a 1 litre microwave-safe glass jug, cover with plastic wrap and cook on HIGH (100%) for 4–5 minutes.
4 Cut the oranges into quarters and then into 2 cm pieces.
5 Return the oranges to the jug and stir into the syrup mixture. Cook, uncovered, on MEDIUM (50–60%) for 30–35 minutes, stirring regularly. The orange rind should be tender.
6 Cool, then spoon the mixture into sterilised jars.

Hint

The true flavour of the orange is in the coloured part of the skin called the zest. This is where the essential flavouring oils are found.

SAUCES

SAUCES

SAUCES

Cooking sauces in a microwave oven is a breeze — there is a little stirring required, no lumps, scorching or boiling over if you use a large jug.

For best results ensure that all ingredients are at room temperature.

Low-fat cooking sometimes results in drier, blander dishes, so innovative sauces will add flavour and moisture. Sweet sauces work well with lean meat dishes and barbequed fish, as well as desserts and cakes.

Custard

Custards are a great way of adding extra calcium to your diet when you tire of yoghurt and milk.

Energy: 265 kJ/60 kCal
Fat: 3 g
Carbohydrate: 7 g
Fibre: –

Serves 3–4 (³/₄ cup)

15 g margarine

1 level tbsp cornflour

³/₄ cup low-fat milk (at room temperature)

2–3 tsp castor sugar

CONVENTIONAL

1 In a medium-sized saucepan heat the margarine on low heat for 1 minute or until the margarine melts.
2 Remove from the heat, and stir in the cornflour, mixing well.
3 Blend in the milk and sugar.
4 Place the saucepan back on a low heat and stir continuously until the sauce has boiled and thickened, about 3 minutes.

MICROWAVE

1 Place the margarine in a microwave-safe glass jug.
2 Leave uncovered, and cook on HIGH (100%) for 45 seconds.
3 Stir in the cornflour and blend well. Leave uncovered, and cook on HIGH (100%) for 30 seconds.
4 Stir in the milk and sugar. Leave uncovered, and cook on HIGH (100%) for 3 minutes, stirring halfway through the cooking time.

Variations

Chocolate custard: Add 1 level tbsp cocoa before stirring in the milk.

Passionfruit custard: Stir in the pulp of 1 passionfruit at the end of the cooking time. Stir well.

Banana custard: Fold 1 sliced banana through warm custard.

Hint

To reheat the custard, place in the microwave oven on MEDIUM (50%), stirring several times.

Orange Custard Sauce

Oranges are a great standby as they stay in peak condition for weeks after they are purchased if stored in a cool dark place — ideal for a touch of sweetness for cakes, desserts and sauces.

Serves 4 (1¼ cups)

½ cup fresh orange juice

½ cup light evaporated milk

2 tsp castor sugar

1 (55 g) egg, well beaten

Energy:	250 kJ/60 kCal
Fat:	1 g
Carbohydrate:	8 g
Fibre:	–

CONVENTIONAL

1 In a medium-sized saucepan heat the orange juice, milk and sugar on high heat for 1–2 minutes, until very warm.

2 Remove from the heat and beat a little of the warm juice mixture into the egg. Pour the egg back into the mixture.

3 Place the saucepan back on a low heat and stir until the sauce has thickened, about 15 minutes. Serve warm or chilled.

MICROWAVE

1 Place the orange juice, milk and sugar in a medium-sized microwave-safe glass jug.

2 Cover with plastic wrap. Cook on HIGH (100%) for 1¾ minutes, until very warm.

3 Remove from the oven and beat a little of the warm juice mixture into the egg. Pour the egg back into the mixture.

4 Re-cover the jug, leaving a vent, and cook on MEDIUM (50–60%) for 3 minutes, stirring every minute until the mixture thickens and is smooth. Serve warm or chilled.

Variation

Use a sweet pink grapefruit, which contains betacarotene and ample vitamin C.

Hints

- *Just one medium-sized orange supplies more than the adult daily requirement of vitamin C. It helps to make collagen, which is essential for healthy skin. It also helps to maintain the body's defences against bacterial infections. As an antioxidant, it may help to ward off or inhibit certain cancers.*

- *Where a recipe calls for both grated zest and juice, always grate the zest before squeezing the juice. This is much easier than the other way round.*

Ricotta Cream

Serves 4

Energy: 320 kJ/75 kCal
Fat: 6 g
Carbohydrate: 1 g
Fibre: –

200 g smooth ricotta

1 tsp sugar

½ tsp vanilla essence

CONVENTIONAL

1 Combine all the ingredients in a mixing bowl. Whisk with an electric beater until the mixture is light and fluffy.
2 Refrigerate until required, and serve cold.

Tangy Citrus Sauce

Crêpes freeze successfully, so you can enjoy a quick snack with this speedy sauce anytime.

Serves 4–6 (1$\frac{1}{3}$ cups)

2 tbsp margarine

2–3 tsp castor sugar

1$\frac{1}{4}$ cups fresh orange juice or tangelo juice

2 tsp cornflour

$\frac{1}{2}$ tsp lemon zest

$\frac{1}{2}$ tsp orange zest

1–2 tbsp Grand Marnier or Cointreau

Energy:	445 kJ/105 kCal
Fat:	8 g
Carbohydrate:	9 g
Fibre:	–

CONVENTIONAL

1 In a medium-sized saucepan heat the margarine and sugar on low heat for 1 minute or until the margarine melts and the sugar dissolves.

2 Remove from the heat and stir in the orange juice and cornflour until smooth.

3 Add the zests, heat to boiling, stirring continuously. Reduce the heat to low and simmer for 10 minutes or until thickened.

4 Stir in the liqueur. Serve over warm crêpes.

MICROWAVE

1 Place the margarine and sugar in a medium-sized microwave-safe glass jug.

2 Leave uncovered and cook on HIGH (100%) for 1 minute.

3 Stir in the orange juice and cornflour until smooth. Add the zests and cover with plastic wrap, leaving a vent. Cook on HIGH (100%) for 3–4 minutes.

4 Stir in the liqueur. Serve over warm crêpes.

Hint

Freeze juicy oranges and tangelos to make this sauce when they are out of season.

Apricot Sauce

The apricot season is a short one, and usually runs from November to December. However, this sauce uses dried apricots, which are available anytime. The sauce can be made ahead of time and stored in the refrigerator.

Energy: 215 kJ/50 kCal
Fat: –
Carbohydrate: 12 g
Fibre: 1 g

Fruit sauces are an excellent way of enhancing the flavour of lean meats and poultry without added fats and oils.

Serves 6 (1²/₃ cups)

1¹/₄ cups natural pineapple juice

¹/₄ cup castor sugar

2 tbsp orange juice

¹/₂ tsp cinnamon

¹/₄ cup water

¹/₂ cup diced dried apricots

CONVENTIONAL

1 In a medium-sized saucepan combine the pineapple juice, sugar, orange juice and cinnamon. Add the water and heat until boiling. Stir in the dried apricots.

2 Reduce the heat, cover and simmer for 10 minutes. Allow to stand for 5 minutes.

3 Pour into a blender and blend until smooth and thickened.

MICROWAVE

1 Place the apricots, pineapple juice, sugar, orange juice and cinnamon in a medium-sized microwave-safe container. Stir in the dried apricots.

2 Cover and cook on HIGH (100%) for 6 minutes, stirring once.

3 Allow to stand for 5 minutes.

4 Pour into a blender and blend until smooth and thickened.

Hint

Serve the sauce warm or chilled over a cake, or use as a glaze for chicken or pork. When selecting fresh apricots, look for yellow to orange fruit.

Fruit Mélange

This is an easy sauce when summer berries or tropical fruit are ripe and sweet.

Serves 6

450 g rhubarb, sliced

1 tbsp cornflour

1/4 cup castor sugar

2 tsp orange zest

1/4 cup water

250 g ripe strawberries and raspberries, hulled, and sliced or diced mango

Energy:	325 kJ/75 kCal
Fat:	–
Carbohydrate:	15 g
Fibre:	4 g

CONVENTIONAL

1 Place the rhubarb in a medium-sized saucepan.
2 Mix the cornflour, sugar and orange zest together. Sprinkle over the rhubarb. Toss lightly to coat.
3 Add the water and heat until boiling. Reduce the heat, cover and simmer for 15 minutes.
4 Add the berries or mango, and cook until just hot, approximately 2 minutes. Serve warm or chilled.

MICROWAVE

1 Place the rhubarb in a large microwave-safe container.
2 Mix the cornflour, sugar and orange zest together. Sprinkle over the rhubarb. Toss lightly to coat.
3 Cover and cook on HIGH (100%) for 6 minutes, stirring once.
4 Add the berries or mango, re-cover, and cook on HIGH (100%) for 2 minutes. Serve warm or chilled.

Hint

Diced mango freezes well, and works well in sauces.

Festive Fruit & Nut Sauce

Good over plum pudding or low-fat icecream.

Makes 2³/₄ cups

¹/₄ cup brown sugar

¹/₂ cup fresh orange juice

¹/₄ cup fresh lemon juice

1 tbsp cornflour

1 tbsp margarine

¹/₄ tsp nutmeg

1 cup water

¹/₄ cup raisins, chopped roughly

¹/₄ cup pecans, chopped

2 tbsp rum or brandy

Energy: 340 kJ/80 kCal
Fat: 4 g
Carbohydrate: 12 g
Fibre: 0.5 g

CONVENTIONAL

1 Combine the sugar, orange and lemon juices, cornflour, margarine, nutmeg and water in a saucepan.
2 Heat to boiling point, stirring constantly. Boil for 1 minute.
3 Add the raisins, pecans and rum. Cover and simmer over low heat for 18 minutes, stirring occasionally. Serve warm or chilled.

MICROWAVE

1 Place the brown sugar, orange and lemon juices, cornflour, margarine, and nutmeg in a large microwave-safe jug.
2 Cover and cook on HIGH (100%) for 5 minutes, stirring twice.
3 Add the raisins, pecans and rum. Recover and cook on MEDIUM (50–60%) for 3 minutes. Stir through and allow to stand for 3 minutes. Serve warm or chilled.

GLOSSARY

Alcohol Used to complement many ingredients in dessert-making. Essences may be substituted.

Baking soda Bicarbonate of soda; used as a leavening agent.

Balsamic vinegar An aged vinegar that comes from Modena. It is slightly sweet and low in sodium. Use over strawberries, in cakes and pickled fruit.

Cassata An Italian-style icecream that has been moulded in contrastingly coloured layers, with dried fruits soaked in brandy or liqueur scattered through.

Castor sugar Superfine sugar.

Cereals Rolled oats, natural muesli, rice bran, All Bran and Weetbix are used.

Cheeses Use low-fat ricotta, parmesan, mozzarella, low-fat cheddar, cottage cheese and low-fat cheese slices.

Coconut milk Made by grating the flesh of fresh coconut very finely, then squeezing the grated meat. Look for low-fat varieties. Also available in canned and powdered form.

Couscous A fine cereal made from wheat, and a North African staple. Cook following the instructions on the pack.

Crumpets A small, spongy yeast cake with holes on the top surface, served toasted or grilled, spread with our recommended toppings.

Custard apple A tropical fruit with green skin and a sweet–sour white flesh.

Dried fruits Choose from unsweetened apricots, mangoes, peaches, pears, pineapple, sultanas, raisins, currants, dates, fruit medley and fruit salad.

Essence A concentrated substance extracted by distillation, infusion or other means.

Filo Very thin sheets of dough made from flour and water. A low-fat replacement for pastry.

Garam masala An Indian blend of ground spices, which may include cinnamon, cloves, cardamom, cumin, nutmeg, coriander and black peppercorns.

Ginger A gnarled and bumpy-looking root that grows in tropical regions. Its flavour is peppery and slightly sweet. Fresh ginger does not have the harshness on the throat that you get with powdered ginger. It will keep in the fridge for about three weeks and freezes well.

Light cream A reduced fat cream.

Lime A green-skinned sour citrus from Mexico that adds a distinctive taste to sweet and savoury dishes.

Marsala A fortified Italian dessert wine.

Mélange A mixture or blend of ingredients.

Milk Use evaporated low-fat milk, skim-milk powder and low-fat milk.

Muffins Traditional English round, flat roll, made with yeast dough, American muffins are made with baking soda/powder in muffin tins.

Multigrain bread Brown bread with added grains.

Nuts Buy them unsalted and use in small quantities. Recommended are peanuts, almonds, pecans, hazelnuts and walnuts.

Oil Spray canola oil and olive oil are used.

Pancetta An Italian bacon. Remove all visible fat.

Pasta Choose from spaghetti, fettuccine, penne, shells, vegeroni and wholemeal pasta.

Pecans A cholesterol-free, low-fat nut that is useful in many areas of 'sweet' cooking.

Pit The act of removing stones from fruit such as prunes, cherries and dates.

Pith The white part of citrus rind that has a bitter taste. Remove before using the rind.

Plain sweet biscuits Ground Granita biscuits are used as a base for slices and cheesecakes.

Polenta Cornmeal.

Pudding A culinary term that usually means dessert, but can also mean a savoury dish.

Quince A fruit that is indigenous to Persia. It is not usually eaten raw, and can be baked, poached or made into jams and preserves.

Rice Basmati, white, brown and arborio (for risotto) rice are used.

Ricotta A smooth, low-fat cheese that is made from the leftover whey from other cheeses. Useful as a stand-in for cream when sweetened or for sour cream when whisked with lemon juice.

Rosewater An extract distilled from water steeped in roses. It is used as a flavouring in the Middle East, the Balkans and India.

Salsa A sauce, which may be sweet or savoury, cooked or fresh.

Soufflé A blown or puffed-up dessert.

Sponge cake A cake whose texture is lightened with separately beaten egg whites, but has no fat and little sugar.

Sweeteners Use sucrulose or aspartaine-based tablet or liquid sweeteners, no-sugar or weight-watchers' jam, as alternatives to sugar and honey.

Tofu Soybean curd that is sold in cakes. It is white, soft and easily digestible, and valued for its nutrient content.

Vanilla bean Vanilla bean is useful for infusing milk with vanilla flavour. Remove the bean after cooking. Use pure essence for custards and desserts.

Yoghurt Natural low-fat yoghurt is a good substitute for sour cream, and flavoured yoghurts for cream.

Zest The coloured part of the skin of citrus fruits where the essential flavouring oils are found.

COOKWARE

Always select the right-sized container for the amount of food being cooked to allow room for the food to sit comfortably or expand, especially with cakes.

If you do not have a turntable in your microwave oven, rotate the food one-third of a turn three times during the cooking time.

Non-stick conventional cookware

Oven tray

Cake pans

Muffin pans

Non-stick baking paper

Microwave cookware

Microwave-safe plastic cookware
700 ml — small
1.5 litres — medium
2.25 or 2.5 litres — large

Microwave-safe glass cookware
500 ml glass jug — small
1 litre (4 cups) glass jug — medium
2 litre (8 cups) glass jug — large

Microwave accessories

Plastic wrap

Non-recycled plain white paper is recommended (not recycled paper towel, which may contain metal fragments). Use this paper over foods, such as baked cakes or when making jams, to absorb excess moisture and to prevent spattering in the oven.

Baking paper

Aluminium foil

INDEX